❀Scandinavian Cooking

ALSO BY BEATRICE OJAKANGAS

The Great Holiday Baking Book

The Great Scandinavian Baking Book

Great Whole Grain Breads

Pot Pies

Quick Breads

Scandinavian Feasts

Beatrice Ojakangas

❋Scandinavian Cooking

University of Minnesota Press   Minneapolis — London

Originally published by HPBooks, 1983

First University of Minnesota Press edition, 2003

Published by the University of Minnesota Press
111 Third Avenue South, Suite 290
Minneapolis, MN 55401-2520
http://www.upress.umn.edu

Library of Congress Cataloging-in-Publication Data

Ojakangas, Beatrice A.
    Scandinavian cooking / Beatrice Ojakangas.—1st University of Minnesota
  Press ed.
        p.   cm.
    ISBN 0-8166-3867-5
    1. Cookery, Scandinavian.   I. Title.
    TX722.A1.O43 2003
    641.5948—dc21

                                                              2003006544

Printed in the United States of America on acid-free paper

12 11 10 09 08 07 06 05 04 03   10 9 8 7 6 5 4 3 2 1

Contents

Smörgåsbords

Acknowledgments

THE AUTHOR IS GRATEFUL to Ruth Kielland, Norwegian Dairies Association; Maria Bøgvald and Jytte Nipper, Danish Dairies; Marja Pekkala of Valio; Finnish Dairies; Marjatta Pauloff, of Arabia of Finland; Kaija Aarikka, of Finland; Gudrun Hoivik, Ivan Nylander, and Lise Gindy, readers for languages; Sally Arntson, Helen Gildseth, Esther Luoma, and friends and relatives who shared ideas and taste-tested recipes and menus for this book.

Special thanks to Maid of Scandinavia, Minneapolis; Kaj Dahl of Scandinavian Center, Los Angeles; Arabia of Finland, Niles, Illinois; and Norwegian and Swedish Imports, Duluth.

Introduction
Scandinavian Cooking

 EACH SCANDINAVIAN COUNTRY has a personality and cuisine of its own. The differences among the four countries represent ways of life fashioned by people adapting themselves to their own climate, natural resources, and terrain.

The backbone of Norwegian cuisine is wonderfully fresh fish and seafood, but it also includes the Norwegians' skill with dairy products. Denmark, the country most influenced by continental cuisine, offers a flower garden of *smørrebrød* and other beautifully presented food. Sweden, the bountiful, is lavish with pork, dairy products, and wonderful baked goods. Sweden gave the world the smörgåsbord, or "bread and butter table." This basic idea has spread throughout Scandinavia, and all kinds of "tables" are set. As you travel, you might begin the day with a breakfast table. When you visit a home, a coffeetable may be waiting for you. If you're invited to lunch, a sandwich table might be served. Or, the food at a cocktail party may be served as a cheese table. Finland has blended influences from Sweden and Russia into its cuisine, but maintains an earthiness native to itself. Karelian pastries of rye and rice, three-meat ragout, rye and barley breads, and fish-filled pies reflect the abundance of whole grains and fish, as well as a knack for baking. Thick soups, hearty breads, fruit puddings, buttery pastries and cookies, cardamom-flavored coffee breads, and spice cakes are healthy and down-to-earth.

The roots of Scandinavian cuisine lie in the area's climate and northern position. In the past, people had to stock supplies for long winters. Today, they find fresh foods in the market from everywhere in the world, although the tastes of the Scandinavians run toward the seasonal. The preservation of meat, fish, vegetables, and fruit has become a fine art. The Vikings developed ways to salt, dehydrate, and cure foods a thousand years ago to prepare for their long voyages.

Although we often think of the Vikings as Norwegians, they came from the entire Scandinavian peninsula. During the Viking Era (A.D. 800 to 1050), borders did not separate Norway, Sweden, Denmark, and Finland. With practically inexhaustible force and energy, Viking plunderers set out on raids, near and far. The word *vikingar* translates to *pirate*. The British Isles and France suffered Viking incursions, and some reports indicate that they made their way as far south as the Mediterranean.

Viking power in Scandinavia was followed by Swedish power and wars between Denmark, Norway, and Sweden. Independence came to Denmark in 1665 and to Norway in 1903. Finland was part of Sweden for six hundred years, until it was conquered by Russia in 1809. In 1917, Finland obtained its freedom.

Norwegian, Swedish, and Danish share linguistic ties as Germanic languages, but Finnish bears no resemblance to them. Finns have always felt their language held them apart—so much so that Bishop Agricola, who brought Christianity to Finland, had to convince the Finns that God could understand Finnish.

Iceland shares cultural and linguistic ties with Norway and Denmark, but its cuisine is not included in this book. Geographically, Finland is not part of Scandinavia, but its past, present, and future have close ties, culturally and historically, with Scandinavia. This book presents the cuisines and customs of those countries that share borders—Norway, Sweden, and Finland—and Denmark, which is almost an extension of Sweden geographically. This region is often, and more accurately, called Fennoscandia.

Because the gulf stream sweeps past the Scandinavian countries and their summer days are long, the climate is temperate enough to raise a variety of food crops. The crops vary somewhat according to the terrain. Denmark, with no mountains, produces field crops and dairy products. The Danes export a wide variety of cheese and pork products. Sweden also depends on dairying and field crops, but has some fishing industry. Norway is mountainous with deep fjords and inlets and relies heavily on its fishing industry, but it also has a very efficient agricultural program. A great deal of cheese is produced for export. Finland exports a large amount of cheese and other food products. These countries produce about the same kinds of food products, but in varying amounts.

The ancient tradition of handicrafts, including woodcarving, metalwork, weaving, embroidery, and rosemaling, is closely related to the aesthetic art of food preparation. Ordinary everyday articles are decorated because they are then considered more enjoyable to use. The handle of a wooden spoon might be carved with fanciful designs. An engraved brooch might be used to hold an apron strap. Cupboard doors and chairs in Norway might be rosemaled—painted or carved with colorful floral or other designs.

Much of Scandinavian cookery has been a well-kept secret. A story is told about a tourist in Oslo who asked a boy, "Where is a good place to eat?" The boy answered, "Best place I've found is right at home." There are fine restaurants in Scandinavia, but they do not serve the kind of food that is eaten every day in homes.

Restaurants serve more European fare than Scandinavian specialties, reflecting French and German influences. In Helsinki, Finland, there are several fine Russian restaurants, though Russian food is seldom seen in the average home. Pizza parlors, hamburger stands, ice cream parlors, and European-style coffeehouses are scattered throughout cities in all countries.

Scandinavian chefs feel free to adapt the foreign classics to include their own available ingredients. This makes eating out rather interesting for a tourist. You might have dishes such as Potatoes Anna or Veal Oscar flavored with allspice and onions—a deviation from the authentic dishes. You may find the same dishes in any of the countries. Names and spellings may differ slightly from one village to the next or from one country to another.

Delicate homemade Scandinavian pastries, grain-rich breads, buttery cookies, sumptuous cakes, homemade cheese, slowly simmered ragouts, light-textured meat and fish loaves, fresh berry desserts, vegetable platters, and seasonal salads are better than those we found in restaurants. In fact, the bakery section of a Scandinavian church bazaar is the best showcase for specialties. The local bakery cannot compete with homemade crisp buttery *sandbakelsers, pepperkaker, goro, rosettes, æbleskiver,* cardamom breads, and other delicacies.

Meals in Scandinavian homes feature the best of what is in season. New potatoes might make a whole meal when they are first in season. A drizzle of butter, perhaps with a sprinkling of fresh dill, is the only adornment. Fresh strawberries are served with cream and sugar, or mixed with whipped cream and generously stuffed between layers of sponge cake, or simply eaten like candy out of a bag.

Scandinavians are master bakers, and everyday cooking is far from bland because they use common ingredients creatively. There is always good bread and something sweet or savory with coffee. Food is usually baked, braised, simmered, or panfried, but seldom deep-fried. Historically, Scandinavians had rendered lard available for deep-frying only after the holiday slaughtering. Today, lard and vegetable shortening are used primarily to deep-fry certain holiday specialties, such as rosettes and fattigman.

Fresh dill is the favorite herb in Scandinavia, but whole peppercorns, whole allspice, dill seeds, fennel, caraway, cardamom, saffron, nutmeg, and cinnamon are used, alone or in combination, to produce new flavors. Dill and ground white pepper might flavor sliced cucumbers or fish; onion and allspice are used to season simmered meats; and orange peel, caraway, fennel, and anise seeds are the classic seasonings for Swedish limpa and Finnish Christmas rye bread. Coffee breads are flavored with the sweet spices: cardamom, saffron, nutmeg, or cinnamon. Almonds are the favorite nut, especially when used as almond paste in fillings for breads, cookies, cakes, and other pastries. Both salt and sugar are used conservatively in Scandinavia.

Arctic cloudberries have a self-preserving quality and can be enjoyed all year without much more preparation than packing them into jars. Lingonberries preserve well, too, and are used much like cranberries. For generations, rose hips, known for their high vitamin C content, have been preserved by nutrition-conscious homemakers.

Cheesemaking has always been important in Scandinavia. Every dairy farm formerly made its own cheese, but today cheesemaking is left to immaculate creameries strategically located throughout all countries. A large percentage of Scandinavian cheese is exported.

A good Scandinavian cook has a flair for color, texture, shape, and stark simplicity in presenting food. Danes tend to lead in fearless combinations: a *smørrebrød*, or open-face sandwich, may be topped with cheese, green pepper, and sliced fresh strawberries! Finns lead in the earthy, chewy, whole-grain bread department. The simplicity of Finnish rye-meal bread magnifies the flavor of the whole-rye grain.

Each of the recipes in this book is labeled with a foreign title and a country of origin, but you may find a dish that is equally important in different countries. Even as a researcher in Scandinavia, it has been impossible for me to find where some dishes originated. Most of these recipes came from friends in Scandinavian countries, gathered during several trips. Other recipes are from friends, relatives, and my personal collection.

As much as possible, I have used ingredients commonly available in supermarkets. Some ingredients are difficult to find substitutes for, so they are described in detail. Special Scandinavian equipment is necessary for some pastries and breads; these materials should be available in Scandinavian specialty cookware shops.

Most of the menus include several choices for each course. Use the menus to give you ideas for entertaining, as well as new thoughts about how to add spark to your family meals.

Scandinavian Equipment and Ingredients

THE FOLLOWING LIST OF TOOLS, equipment, and special ingredients will help to make Scandinavian dishes authentic. These items are available at Scandinavian specialty cookware stores and at fine grocery or kitchen stores.

Equipment

Æbleskiver or Munk's Pan: A heavy cast-iron or cast-aluminum pan with round cups that is used to make ball-shaped Danish pancakes, sometimes called *munks* or doughnuts. The pan will season itself with use, but nonstick spray, vegetable shortening, butter, or lard is generally used in the cups at each baking. As the batter cooks, it rises. As one side bakes, a filling of chopped apple, applesauce, or jam may be spooned into the center, and extra batter is then added to enclose the filling. A metal knitting needle or wooden skewer is used to turn the pancake ball over. Immediately after each use, wash the pan in warm sudsy water; rinse and dry. See Danish Pancake Balls (page 224).

Goro Iron: Cast-iron or cast-aluminum, this hinged, patterned Norwegian cookie iron is used to make thin, flat rectangles that break into three cookies. Brush the inside of the iron with nonstick spray, butter, or vegetable shortening when baking the first few cookies. Immediately after each use, wash the iron in warm, sudsy water; rinse and dry. To store the iron, place folded paper towels between the top and bottom plates. See Cardamom Crackers (page 110).

Hardtack or Knäckebröd Rolling Pin: This wooden rolling pin has a hob-nail roller used to make a pattern in the dough when rolling out flatbreads. See Rye and Wheat Flatbread (page 47).

Heart-Shape Waffle Iron: This cast-iron or cast-aluminum waffle iron is shaped like five small hearts. Some irons have nonstick finishes. Some are electric, but traditionally they are heated on the stove top. Some are equipped with a cradle support for easy turning. Brush both top and bottom plates with butter or vegetable shortening or nonstick spray each time you add batter. Immediately after each use, wash the iron in warm, sudsy water; rinse and dry. To store the iron, place folded paper towels between the top and bottom plates. See Heart-Shape Waffles (page 12) or use any waffle batter.

Karelian Rolling Pin: This long, slender, Finnish rolling pin is usually made of light birch. The pin is thicker in the center, making it easier to spin the dough as it is rolled out. See Karelian Pies (page 165).

Kransekake or Ring Pans: Set of eighteen individual rings or six pans with three rings. Ring sizes vary from 2⅜ inches to 7¾ inches in diameter. Grease each ring before using or coat with nonstick spray. Used to make the towering Norwegian or Scandinavian celebration cake. Immediately after each use, wash the rings in warm, sudsy water; rinse and dry.

Krumkaker or Krumkake Iron: Hinged, patterned, cast-iron or cast-aluminum Norwegian iron used to make thin, round, five- to six-inch cookies. Use nonstick spray, vegetable shortening, butter, or lard each time the pan is used. It will season itself. Too much butter or shortening will run out onto the stove. Immediately after each use, wash the iron in warm, sudsy water; rinse and dry. To store the iron, place folded paper towels between the top and bottom plates. See Krumbcakes (page 280).

Lefse Rolling Pin: Norwegian rolling pin with long grooves along either the length of the roller or around the roller. Used for rolling out Norwegian *lefse,* a thin flatbread baked on a griddle. See Potato Flatbread (page 45), Rye and Wheat Flatbread (page 47), and Mrs. Olson's Flour Lefse (page 226).

Plättar or Plette Pan: Cast-iron or cast-aluminum Swedish pan with shallow, round indentations for making thin pancakes about three inches in diameter. Use nonstick spray, vegetable shortening, butter, or lard each time the pan is used. It will season itself. Immediately after each use, wash the pan in warm, sudsy water; rinse and dry. See Swedish Pancakes (page 13).

Rosette Irons: Used to make fragile deep-fried patty shells or cookie-like pastries. Usually comes as a set of three or four irons with a removable handle. Additional irons are available. Some handles have two arms and will cook two designs at one time. Immediately after each use, wash the irons in warm, sudsy water; rinse and dry. See Rosettes (page 281).

Sandbakelser, Sandbakkel, or Tart Tins: Fluted, slant-sided Swedish tartlet tins commonly used in all Scandinavian countries to make tart shells or cookies. The tins come in several sizes. Sets usually include from twelve to eighteen tins. Immediately after each use, wash the tins in warm, sudsy water; rinse and dry. Stack one inside another to store. See Savory Tartlets (page 125) and Butter Cookie Shells (page 276).

Special Foods and Ingredients

If some of the following foods are not available in your local supermarket, check local specialty food stores.

Cardamom: Aromatic spice commonly used in pastries and yeast breads. Cardamom pods and ground cardamom are available in most well-stocked supermarkets. Because it loses its pungency quickly after being ground, commercially ground cardamom has very little flavor. It is best to purchase whole, white, papery, cardamom pods. Use a mortar and pestle to open the pods and remove the seeds. Blow gently on the pod and seeds to remove the pieces of pod, then crush the small black aromatic seeds using the mortar and pestle, or a spice or coffee grinder. Or place the seeds between sheets of plastic or waxed paper and crush by pounding with a mallet or hammer.

Cloudberries: These yellow Arctic berries resemble raspberries in shape with lots of seeds. Preserved berries are available in jars. Used for cake and tart fillings, as well as dessert sauces.

Lingonberries: Small, round red berries, tart and much like cranberries in flavor. In some supermarkets, they can be purchased in bulk, sweetened or unsweetened, or preserved in jars. Lingonberries are served with meat, game, and poultry dishes.

Pearl Sugar: A confectionery sugar used for decorating coffee breads and cookies. The texture is coarse and can be simulated by coarsely crushing sugar cubes. Imported from Sweden.

Pickled Herring: There is a wide variety of herring packed in wine sauce, dill sauce, or brine. It may be cut in tidbits, chunks, or fillets. Herring is usually served directly from the container, but may be seasoned and spiced.

Swedish Anchovies or Baltic Sprats: Do not confuse with smaller, saltier, Portuguese-style anchovies. Available in Scandinavian fish markets or Scandinavian specialty stores. They must be refrigerated. Fillets are available in flat, three-ounce tins. Also available whole, packed in jars of brine.

Salted or Brined Whole Herring: Any herring packed in salt brine can be used in recipes calling for salted herring. Before using, soak them in cold water for several hours to remove excess salt. Available in delicatessens and fish stores, as well as Scandinavian specialty foods markets.

Swedish Brown Beans (Bruna Bönor): Small, oval, Swedish-grown brown beans. Pinto beans or Great Northern beans may be substituted, but are not the same in flavor or texture. Dried beans are available in Scandinavian specialty stores.

Veal Terrine (Sylta): Shredded meat set in jellied beef broth. Served as a cold-cut during holidays. Can be purchased sliced or in bulk in Scandinavian specialty meat markets.

❁Breakfasts and Brunches

Farmhouse Brunch

MENU

Buttered Potato Soup

Swedish Bacon Bake

Danish Pastries (pages 251–63)

Country Oat Loaf (page 250)

Mushroom-Stuffed Tomatoes

Fresh Fruit in Season

Coffee, Tea, Milk, Juices

SEVERAL YEARS AGO in the home of relatives in Western Finland, I admired a mammoth brick range with its bread-baking oven. We sat at the painted wooden kitchen table, enjoying fresh-baked *Pulla,* a cardamom-flavored coffee bread. Behind us ticked an hourglass-shaped grandfather clock. Since then, because of a desire for the new and modern, many people have removed the old brick ranges and ovens and replaced them with modern electric ranges. I was happy to learn recently that some of the lovely old farmhouses are being renovated and the big brick ranges, complete with bread ovens, are being restored.

Illalla perunavoi, aamulla klapsakkaa, ei emäntä kulta siillä jaksakkaa. "In the evening, mashed potatoes; in the morning, potato broth. No, my dear wife, I cannot work on just that." This old quote from a Finnish farmer to his wife tells us several things about the past. The hardworking farmer needed substantial food—meat and potatoes—for his breakfast. And the thrifty Finnish wife was using creativity with the simplest of ingredients—leftover potatoes and milk.

Many Scandinavian farmers now supplement their income with jobs away from their fields and forests. Their spouses may also be working. Meal patterns have changed from the traditional early morning coffee, breakfast at 11:00 A.M., coffee at 4:00 P.M., and dinner at 5:00 P.M. Today, because of working away from the farm, they have three meals—breakfast, lunch, and dinner.

In the summer, whether at home or visiting friends or relatives, breakfast is simple. You may have a bowl of fresh berries from the garden or from a colorful open-market stall. The fruit is served with bread, butter, and coffee. In the winter, the fruit may be a bowl of preserved cloudberries, stewed prunes, applesauce, or fresh lingonberries—available all year in Scandinavia.

The menu here combines elements from several Scandinavian countries. Today, it is not uncommon for a traveler to find Norwegian foods in Finland and Danish or Swedish foods in Norway. There is a free exchange of recipes and ideas throughout Scandinavia and the world, mostly due to the great number of food-related magazines available.

Buttered Potato Soup

Klapsakkaa—Finland

Make this creamy soup with last night's potatoes and serve it steaming hot in mugs.

2 cups mashed potatoes
4 cups milk
2 cups half-and-half
Salt and pepper to taste
Dash ground allspice
About 2 tablespoons chopped fresh parsley
About 4 teaspoons butter

In a medium saucepan, beat potatoes and milk with a whisk until smooth. Stir in half-and-half. Stir over medium heat until soup barely comes to a boil. Add salt and pepper to taste. Sprinkle top with a dash of allspice. Ladle into individual bowls or mugs. Garnish each with parsley and ½ teaspoon butter. Serve immediately. Makes 8 servings.

Swedish Bacon Bake

Äggkaka—Sweden

Prepare this omelet the night before and bake it at the last minute.

1 pound sliced bacon
½ pound mushrooms, sliced
3 tablespoons butter, if desired
2 tablespoons cornstarch
2 cups half-and-half
18 eggs
1 teaspoon salt
½ teaspoon dried leaf tarragon
1½ cups shredded Emmentaler or Jarlsberg cheese (6 ounces)

Butter a shallow 2- to 3-quart casserole dish; set aside. Cut bacon slices in half. In a large skillet, cook bacon over medium heat until crisp. Drain on paper towels. Increase heat to high. Pour off all but about 3 tablespoons bacon drippings. Sauté mushrooms in bacon drippings until mushrooms are lightly browned, about 3 minutes. Or, if desired, melt butter in a large skillet; sauté mushrooms in melted butter. Stir in cornstarch until evenly distributed. Slowly stir in half-and-half until blended. Cook and stir until thickened. In a large bowl, beat eggs until blended. Stir in 1 or 2 cups mushroom mixture. Stir egg mixture into remaining mushroom mixture. Scramble over medium heat just until eggs begin to set; do not cook completely. Stir in salt and tarragon. Pour partially cooked egg mixture into prepared casserole dish. Sprinkle cheese over top. Overlap cooked bacon slices around edge. Cover and refrigerate overnight, if desired, or bake immediately. To bake immediately, preheat oven to 300°F (150°C). Bake 30 minutes or until casserole is heated through and cheese is melted. To bake after being refrigerated, preheat oven to 300°F (150°C); bake 45 minutes. Makes 8 to 10 generous servings.

Mushroom-Stuffed Tomatoes

Täytetty Tomatit—Finland

A colorful and satisfying brunch dish.

>   8 medium tomatoes
>   2 cups finely chopped mushrooms
>   1 cup whipping cream
>   1 cup finely chopped sweet onion
>   3 tablespoons fresh lemon juice
>   2 tablespoons Dijon mustard
>   ½ teaspoon ground white pepper
>   ½ to 1 teaspoon salt
>   Parsley sprigs or leaf lettuce for garnish, if desired

Cut a ¼-inch slice off bottom of each tomato. Reserve slices; keep with tomatoes from which they were cut. Scoop seeds and pulp from center of tomatoes. Arrange tomatoes and reserved slices, cut-side down, on paper towels to drain. Wrap mushrooms in paper towels to remove as much moisture as possible. In a medium bowl, whip cream until soft peaks form. Fold in dry mushrooms, onion, lemon juice, mustard, white pepper, and salt to taste. Spoon into tomatoes. Insert reserved slices vertically into mushroom mixture. Garnish with parsley or lettuce, if desired. Arrange stuffed tomatoes on a platter. Makes 8 servings.

Summertime Garden Breakfast

MENU

Raspberry Nectar

Samsøe Soufflé

Heart-Shape Waffles

or

Swedish Pancakes

Whipped Cream, Fresh Berries, or Other Fruit

Milk, Fruit Juice, Coffee, Tea

SCANDINAVIAN LONG SUMMER DAYS have a few hours of silver twilight that mark the nighttime. By two in the morning, birds are awake and calling each other, their resonant voices somehow amplified in the wooded surroundings. In gardens, roses bloom among the irises, peonies, and lupines. A Scandinavian summer garden is an inspiring place to have a leisurely breakfast.

In the summer, one might be invited to a midnight coffee party that continues until breakfast. The party is usually held at the host's summertime retreat—a cabin or mountain hut—away from the bustle of city life. Businesses often close for an entire month to let their employees fully enjoy summer. It is an inconvenient time to try to do business, but a wonderful time to have friends with a summer house.

Berries and garden vegetables ripen quickly in the intensity of long summer days. Dairy herds are at their peak production and supplies of dairy products are plentiful.

When the day will be spent at home, most Scandinavians begin their day with early morning coffee and a piece of cardamom-perfumed bread, a crisp rusk, or a slice of rye bread topped with a shaving of cheese. On a Scandinavian farm, breakfast is served at about 11:00 A.M. This full, hot meal usually includes boiled potatoes, a meat dish, bread, cheese, and perhaps a fruit pudding for dessert.

Heart-Shape Waffles are a many-season favorite in Norway, but a special spring and summer treat. In Sweden, these waffles are traditionally served on Lady Day, March 25—formally known as Annunciation Day. This is exactly nine months before Christmas. These special waffles are delicious served hot, but are usually served cold. Be sure to cover them with plastic wrap and refrigerate them so they won't dry out before you serve them. No matter how much cream is in the batter, Scandinavians still prefer their waffles served with whipped cream and berries!

Raspberry Nectar

Hallonsaft—Sweden

After adding water, serve this clear red nectar over ice in stemmed glasses.

4 quarts red raspberries
2 cups white wine vinegar
2 cups water
About 4 cups sugar

In a large glass jar or bowl, combine raspberries, vinegar, and water. Let stand overnight. Wash 4 pint jars in hot soapy water; rinse. Keep hot. Prepare self-sealing lids as manufacturer directs. Pour raspberry mixture into a large saucepan. Stirring occasionally, bring to a boil over medium heat; boil 1 minute. Line a strainer with several layers of damp cheesecloth or a damp muslin towel; place over a large bowl. Pour mixture into lined strainer. Let juice drip through lined strainer; do not squeeze. Measure juice; return juice to pan. For each cup of juice, add ¾ cup sugar. Stirring constantly, bring to a boil over medium heat; boil 10 minutes. Pour juice into 1 hot jar at a time, leaving ¼ inch headspace. Wipe rim of jar with a clean damp cloth. Attach lid. Place in a water-bath canner or a pot large enough to hold jars covered with boiling water. Fill and close remaining jars. After water comes to a boil, begin timing. Process 15 minutes, adding 1 minute for each 1,000 feet of altitude above sea level. Cool on a rack, away from drafts, 10 to 12 hours. Do not tighten rings of self-sealing lids. Check lids for seal. If jars did not seal, store in refrigerator. To serve, add ¼ cup nectar to 1 pint water. Adjust amount of nectar to taste. Pour over ice cubes in drinking glasses. Makes 4 pints.

Samsøe Soufflé

Samsøsouffle—Denmark

You can prepare this soufflé, freeze it, then bake it later—but it will have a coarse texture.

1 cup half-and-half
¼ cup all-purpose flour
2 tablespoons butter
1 cup shredded Samsøe or Tybo cheese (4 ounces)
½ teaspoon salt
¼ teaspoon white pepper
4 eggs, separated
⅛ teaspoon cream of tartar

Butter a 1- to 1½-quart soufflé dish; set aside. In a medium saucepan, combine half-and-half and flour. Beat with a whisk until smooth. Over medium heat, stir with a whisk until mixture comes to a boil. Add butter. Cook and stir until mixture thickens. Stir in cheese, salt, and white pepper. In a small bowl, beat egg yolks until blended. Stir in about ½ cup cheese sauce. Stir egg yolk mixture into remaining cheese sauce; set aside. In a medium bowl, beat egg whites until frothy. Add cream of tartar; continue beating until whites form short, soft, but distinctive peaks; tips of peaks will bend over. Fold into cheese sauce. Pour cheese mixture into prepared dish. Bake or cover and freeze. To bake immediately, preheat oven to 375°F (190°C). Bake 30 to 35 minutes or until puffed and golden. Soufflé will be soft in center. To bake after freezing, preheat oven to 350°F (175°C). Remove cover from soufflé dish; place frozen soufflé in preheated oven. Bake 45 to 60 minutes. Makes 4 servings.

Heart-Shape Waffles

Fløtevafler—Norway

Delicious hot, but usually served cold.

5 eggs
½ cup sugar
½ teaspoon salt
1 teaspoon ground cardamom
1 cup all-purpose flour
1 cup dairy sour cream, stirred
¼ cup unsalted butter, melted
Fresh lingonberries or other berries or fruit
Whipped cream

In large bowl of electric mixer, beat eggs and sugar on high speed until mixture forms ribbons when beaters are lifted from bowl, about 10 minutes. Beat in salt and cardamom. Sprinkle flour over surface of batter. Use a rubber spatula to fold in flour, then fold in sour cream and butter. Let mixture stand 10 minutes. Preheat heart-shape waffle iron according to manufacturer's directions. Pour about ¾ cup batter onto center of waffle iron. Close top; bake 2 to 3 minutes on each side over medium heat until waffle is golden and crisp. Serve immediately with berries or other fruit and whipped cream. Or, cool waffles on a rack and serve cold. Makes about 8 waffles or 40 heart-shape pieces.

Swedish Pancakes

Plättar—Sweden

So light that Swedes say they should "fly off the griddle."

1 egg
¾ cup milk
¼ teaspoon salt
½ cup all-purpose flour
1 teaspoon baking powder
1 tablespoon sugar
2 tablespoons butter, melted
Lingonberry jam or other jam or jelly
Dairy sour cream

Preheat plättar pan (page XVI) over medium heat. In a large bowl, beat egg; stir in milk, salt, flour, baking powder, and sugar until batter is smooth. Stir in melted butter. Grease cups in hot pan with shortening or butter. Spoon 2 rounded tablespoons batter into each greased cup. Cook about 1 minute on each side or until golden brown. Serve immediately with jam or jelly and sour cream. Makes 20 pancakes.

If a recipe calls for room-temperature eggs and yours are cold, fill a bowl with hot tap water. Immerse the eggs in the water and let stand three to four minutes. Separated egg whites and yolks can be warmed by placing them in bowls over warm water.

❀Smørrebrød—
Open-Face Sandwiches

Smørrebrød Sampler

MENU

FIRST COURSE:

Onion and Herring Smørrebrød

Cream Cheese and Salmon Smørrebrød

Dilled Shrimp Smørrebrød

MAIN COURSE:

Chicken and Cucumber Smørrebrød

Beef and Onion Smørrebrød

Roast Pork Smørrebrød

Egg and Caviar Smørrebrød

DESSERT COURSE:

Red Berry Pudding

or

Danish Rum Cream

Vanilla Wreaths (page 271)

Caroline's Apple Cake

Danish Beer, Schnapps, Coffee, Tea

SHRIMP AND OTHER SHELLFISH are abundant along the seacoasts of Scandinavia. One can walk along the pier of a seacoast village in Norway or Denmark, buy a sack of freshly cooked shrimp, and shell them as you would peanuts. Pop the delicious morsels into your mouth, then drop the shells into the water for scavenger fish to devour. They also make excellent *smørrebrød*.

Although smørrebrød originated in Denmark, they can become a sampling of Scandinavian flavors. Herring, onion, salted salmon, shrimp, beef, and many other ingredients are classic smørrebrød fare. Smørrebrød have become popular throughout Scandinavia. Tourists can walk into any coffee bar and find simple or elaborate open-face sandwiches.

When you plan a whole meal of smørrebrød, follow the pattern for a regular menu, planning two, three, or four courses. Start with a first course of fish, followed with meat or poultry for the main course. Smørrebrød may be served for all courses, even dessert. However, in Denmark, dessert is usually a fruit or cream pudding with a cookie, Danish pastry, or cream cake. Dessert smørrebrød may be cheese, nuts, and fruit, alone or in combination. Schnapps or aquavit, followed by beer as a chaser, is appropriate even at lunch.

This menu offers flexibility. Choose one or more of the smørrebrød from each course. Serve each course separately. Or, offer all of the smørrebrød at the same luncheon. For a cooperative effort, ask each guest to bring one smørrebrød to be sampled. All the smørrebrød can be made ahead and re-frigerated overnight.

How to Make Smørrebrød

1. Use compact loaves of homemade or commercial bread that hold their shape when cut. Dark breads, firm pumpernickels, or firm slices of French bread are best. Day-old bread is better than freshly baked bread. Slice all dark breads ¼ to ⅜ inch thick. Remove the crusts. Slice French bread about ½ inch thick. Do not remove the crusts.
2. Arrange slices of bread on a flat surface. Butter each slice, covering to all edges. This will prevent moist toppings from soaking through. Add each topping and garnish to all slices of bread before adding the next topping or garnish.
3. Place a leaf of lettuce on one end or corner of the buttered bread, gathering it so it takes up little space. The lettuce should not cover the entire slice of bread.
4. Cover remaining bread with thinly sliced fish, meat, or vegetables.
5. Garnish with red and green vegetables or fruits, such as radish slices, parsley sprigs, watercress, bean or alfalfa sprouts, tomato pieces or wedges, onion rings, cucumber twists, or orange or lemon twists.

Onion and Herring Smørrebrød

Sild med Løg—Denmark

Herring and onion smørrebrød is the favorite of all combinations!

4 slices Danish Pumpernickel (page 247) or other rye bread
4 teaspoons butter, softened
1 jar herring fillets in wine sauce (8 ounces)
1 medium, sweet onion, cut in thin rings
8 thin tomato wedges
Watercress or parsley

Cut crusts from bread. Spread 1 teaspoon butter on each slice of bread, covering completely. Cut each buttered slice in half crosswise; trim to make 4 x 2-inch rectangles. Drain fish; cut in 1-inch strips. Top each piece of bread with one-eighth of herring, placing fish smooth-side up. Top each with several onion rings and 1 tomato wedge. Garnish each with watercress or parsley. Makes 8 sandwiches.

Cream Cheese and Salmon Smørrebrød
Flødeost med Laks—Denmark

Use your own homemade Salted Salmon (page 209) or purchase it at a delicatessen.

4 slices Danish Pumpernickel (page 247) or other rye bread
4 teaspoons butter
2 ounces cream cheese, softened
3 ounces thinly sliced smoked or salted salmon
16 paper-thin cucumber slices

Cut crusts from bread. Spread 1 teaspoon butter on each piece of bread, covering completely. Cut each buttered slice in half crosswise; trim to make 4 x 2-inch rectangles. Spread each with cream cheese, covering completely. Top each with salmon, laying salmon flat. Top each with 2 cucumber slices, gathering slices in a mound. Makes 8 sandwiches.

Dilled Shrimp Smørrebrød

Rejer i Trængsel—Denmark

Purchase frozen tiny shrimp that are already cooked.

2 thin lemon slices
3 tablespoons butter, softened
8 slices French bread
1 cup mayonnaise
1 teaspoon dried dill weed
8 small butter or leaf lettuce leaves
½ pound tiny cooked shrimp, thawed if frozen
8 thin tomato wedges
8 tiny parsley sprigs

Cut lemon slices in quarters; set aside. Spread about 1 teaspoon butter on each slice of bread, covering completely. Spread each with 2 tablespoons mayonnaise; sprinkle each with dill weed. Place 1 lettuce leaf on end of each slice of bread. Divide shrimp among sandwiches, mounding on top of mayonnaise and lettuce. Garnish each with a tomato wedge, a piece of lemon, and a parsley sprig. Makes 8 sandwiches.

Chicken and Cucumber Smørrebrød

Kylling med Agurke—Denmark

Poached chicken breast and cucumbers on buttered bread make a tasty open-face sandwich.

    1 tablespoon sugar
    1 teaspoon salt
    ¼ cup distilled white vinegar
    ¼ cup water
    1 European-style cucumber or other cucumber (8 inches), thinly sliced
    Poached Chicken Breasts (below)
    4 slices Danish Pumpernickel (page 247) or other rye bread
    4 teaspoons butter, softened
    4 butter or leaf lettuce leaves
    4 thin tomato slices or wedges
    4 bacon slices, cooked crisp

Poached Chicken Breasts

    1 chicken breast, halved, skinned, boned
    ½ cup dry white wine
    ½ cup water
    1 teaspoon pickling spices

In a medium bowl, combine sugar, salt, vinegar, and water. Stir in cucumber. Refrigerate 30 to 60 minutes. Prepare Poached Chicken Breasts; set aside to cool. Cut crusts from bread. Spread 1 teaspoon butter on each slice of bread, covering completely. Gather lettuce leaves in ruffles. Place each ruffled leaf on 1 end of a slice of bread. Place one-fourth of poached chicken slices on uncovered portion of bread. Drain cucumbers on paper towels; arrange one-fourth of drained cucumbers on each sandwich. Garnish each with a tomato slice or wedge and bacon. Makes 4 sandwiches.

Poached Chicken Breasts

Place chicken breast halves in an 8-inch skillet. Add wine, water, and pickling spices. Bring to a boil, then simmer over low heat 20 minutes or until meat is firm but not hard. Drain; let cool. Use a sharp knife to slice diagonally across grain, as thinly as possible.

Beef and Onion Smørrebrød

Oksesteg med Løg—Denmark

The Danes use leftover beef in sandwiches, but the Swedes use it on a smörgåsbord.

8 slices Danish Pumpernickel (page 247) or other rye bread
8 teaspoons butter, softened
⅓ cup Dijon mustard
8 thin slices rare roast beef (about ½ pound)
8 teaspoons dairy sour cream
½ cup canned crisp-fried onions, crumbled
8 thin tomato wedges
8 parsley or watercress sprigs

Cut crusts from bread. Spread 1 teaspoon butter on each slice of bread, covering completely. Spread each generously with mustard. Place 1 slice roast beef on top of each, gathering or ruffling so beef covers bread but does not extend over sides. Top each beef slice with 1 teaspoon sour cream. Sprinkle with crumbled onions; top with a tomato wedge. Garnish with parsley or watercress. Makes 8 sandwiches.

Roast Pork Smørrebrød

Flæskesteg—Denmark

Pork, pickled cabbage, and prunes—who but the Danes would put them together?

8 slices Danish Pumpernickel (page 247) or other rye bread
8 teaspoons butter, softened
8 small butter or leaf lettuce leaves
8 thin slices roast pork (about ½ pound)
½ cup canned sweet-sour red cabbage, chilled and drained
8 cooked prunes, pitted
8 thin slices peeled orange
8 parsley sprigs

Cut crusts from bread. Spread 1 teaspoon butter on each slice of bread, covering completely. Press a small lettuce leaf onto 1 end of each buttered slice. Fold and ruffle sliced pork to cover bread completely. Top each with 1 tablespoon cabbage and 1 pitted prune. Cut each orange slice from outside edge to center; twist. Place 1 orange twist on top of each sandwich. Garnish each with parsley. Makes 8 sandwiches.

Egg and Caviar Smørrebrød

Æg med Kaviar—Denmark

It is traditional to cut the crusts from most breads to give the smørrebrød an even edge.

> 4 slices Danish Pumpernickel (page 247) or other rye bread
> 4 teaspoons butter
> 2 tablespoons mayonnaise
> 4 hard-cooked eggs, sliced
> 2 tablespoons red or black lumpfish, salmon, or sturgeon caviar
> Parsley

Cut crusts from bread. Spread 1 teaspoon butter on each slice of bread, covering completely. Cut each buttered slice in half crosswise or into 4 x 2-inch pieces. Spread each with mayonnaise, then top with egg slices. Dot each egg slice with caviar. Garnish with parsley. Makes 8 sandwiches.

Red Berry Pudding

Rødgrød—Denmark

This interesting berry pudding has a jelly-like consistency.

> 1 pound fresh or frozen unsweetened raspberries, strawberries,
>   blackberries, or boysenberries
> About 4 cups water
> ⅓ cup cornstarch
> 1 cup sugar
> Pinch of salt
> ¼ cup sliced almonds, toasted
> 1 cup whipping cream

In a medium saucepan, combine berries and 4 cups water. Bring to a boil. Simmer over low heat 5 minutes. Place a strainer over a medium bowl. Pour berry mixture into strainer; press with the back of a spoon to remove as much pulp as possible. Discard seeds. Measure juice and pulp. If necessary, add water to make 5 cups. In a small bowl, combine cornstarch with ⅔ cup juice from pulp, making a thin paste. Pour remaining juice and pulp into saucepan; bring to a boil over medium heat, stirring occasionally. Stir in sugar, salt, and cornstarch paste. Stirring vigorously with a wooden spoon to keep pudding smooth, cook until thickened. Cover pan; set aside to cool 20 to 30 minutes. Pour cooled pudding into a serving bowl. Sprinkle with sliced almonds. Serve immediately or cover bowl with plastic wrap and refrigerate until served. Pour whipping cream into a small pitcher. Serve pudding warm or cold, with cream. Makes 8 servings.

Danish Rum Cream

Romfromage—Denmark

Rum-flavored desserts became popular when Denmark had colonies in the West Indies.

1 envelope unflavored gelatin (¼ ounce)
¼ cup cold water
2 cups milk
4 egg yolks
¼ cup sugar
¼ teaspoon salt
1 cup whipping cream
2 tablespoons rum or ¼ teaspoon rum extract

Stir gelatin into cold water; set aside to soften 5 minutes. In a medium saucepan, heat milk until surface begins to shimmer. In a small bowl, beat egg yolks, sugar, and salt until fluffy. Stir ¼ cup hot milk into sugar mixture. Whisking constantly, pour sugar mixture into remaining hot milk. Cook and stir 2 minutes or until mixture thickens enough to coat a spoon. Place saucepan with milk mixture in a larger saucepan or sink. Pour cold water into outer container. Stir gelatin into milk mixture. Replacing cold water in outer container as necessary, stir occasionally as milk mixture chills and thickens. Whip cream; fold into chilled milk mixture. Stir in rum or rum extract. Pour into a serving bowl. Cover and refrigerate at least 2 hours before serving. Makes 6 servings.

Caroline's Apple Cake
Karolines Æblekage—Denmark

Apple cakes similar to this are popular all over Scandinavia.

    4 to 5 medium Golden Delicious apples
    ¾ cup butter, room temperature
    ¾ cup sugar
    3 eggs, room temperature
    ¼ teaspoon salt
    1 teaspoon vanilla extract
    1½ cups all-purpose flour
    2 tablespoons butter, melted
    2 tablespoons sugar

Butter an 11-inch tart pan with a removable bottom or a 9-inch square cake pan; set aside. Peel and halve apples. Use a melon baller or a teaspoon to remove cores. Preheat oven to 425°F (220°C). In a large bowl, cream ¾ cup butter and ¾ cup sugar. Beat in eggs, salt, and vanilla until light and fluffy. Stir in flour to make a stiff batter. Spread batter in prepared pan. Arrange apples on a flat surface, cut-side down. Cut parallel horizontal incisions almost all the way through each apple half, 1/16 to 1/8 inch apart. Do not cut all the way through. Press apple halves, core-side down, into batter. Brush apples with 2 tablespoons melted butter; sprinkle with 2 tablespoons sugar. Bake 30 minutes or until apples are tender and cake is golden brown. Makes 6 to 8 servings.

Smørrebrød to Honor Danish Arts

MENU

FIRST COURSE:

Danish Apple Soup

MAIN COURSE:

Sardine and Onion Smørrebrød

Smoked Salmon Smørrebrød

Turkey-Lingonberry Smørrebrød

Ham and Egg Smørrebrød

DESSERT COURSE:

Cheese and Grape Smørrebrød

Cheese and Strawberry Smørrebrød

Havarti and Walnut Smørrebrød

Schnapps, Beer, Coffee, Tea, Fruit Juice

AS OUR TOUR BUS PULLED THROUGH the elephant-pillar gates of Carlsberg brewery in Copenhagen, our guide explained that the firm was owned by the state. All profits from the brewery go toward furthering the arts in Denmark. In her guttural voice, she advised us, "When you lift your glass of Danish beer, you can always make it a toast to the arts in Denmark!"

What you serve as a drink in Scandinavia depends on whether the person is driving an automobile. There are strict rules that forbid anyone who has had even a drop of anything alcoholic to drive. For this reason, all parties have a nonalcoholic beverage for guests. Those who are walking or are passengers may choose beer or wine. Mineral water, milk, buttermilk, or fruit juices are usually the other choices. Coffee is served after dessert and is rarely, if ever, served with a meal.

Soup is often the predinner drink in Scandinavia, served in a mug before you sit down. Danes often surprise us with new ideas. Apples form the basis of the creamy, curry-flavored soup in the menu here. It is served as a separate first course.

Smørrebrød, literally translated, means buttered *(smør)* bread *(brød)*. This Danish open-face sandwich is a culinary cross between a sandwich and a salad. It is a small meal by itself when topped with vegetables, meat, fish, poultry, or cheese. It is always eaten on a plate, with a knife and fork, not out-of-hand.

Smørrebrød can be served in different ways. In one Danish home, all ingredients for smørrebrød are served separately. Guests make their own open-face sandwiches. In another home, several types of completed smørrebrød are arranged on a tray. Guests make their own selection. Another method is to have three different smørrebrød on each person's plate. If you want a meal to last a long time, serve the smørrebrød one variety at a time.

Prepared in full, this menu offers an impressive array of colorful smørrebrød. You may want to select one to four varieties from each course and increase the recipes from four to twelve servings.

Danish Apple Soup

Æblesuppe—Denmark

In Denmark, apples are sometimes used as vegetables in soups and salads.

1½ pounds cooking apples (6 to 8), such as Granny Smith or
   Golden Delicious
5 whole cloves
Water
1 tablespoon lemon juice
2 cups white wine, white grape juice, or water
2 tablespoons cornstarch
1 to 2 teaspoons curry powder
½ cup whipping cream
3 tablespoons sugar
1 teaspoon butter
⅛ teaspoon salt

Wash and peel apples, reserving peel. Immediately combine peelings, cloves, and water to cover in a large saucepan. Over medium-low heat, simmer 30 minutes. While peelings simmer, core and slice apples. Sprinkle with lemon juice to prevent darkening. Place a strainer over a medium bowl. Pour peeling mixture into strainer. Discard peelings and cloves; return broth to saucepan. Add apple slices and 2 cups wine, juice, or water. Simmer over low heat 30 minutes or until apples are tender. Puree apple mixture in a blender, adding cornstarch and curry powder during processing. Pour pureed mixture into saucepan. Stir in cream, sugar, butter, and salt. Bring to a gentle boil over medium heat. Cook and stir until thickened. Serve hot. Makes 6 servings.

Sardine and Onion Smørrebrød

Sardin med Løg—Denmark

Convenient canned sardines from Denmark or Norway make this smørrebrød quick to prepare.

    4 slices Danish Pumpernickel (page 247) or other rye bread
    4 teaspoons butter, softened
    1 can sardines (3 to 4 ounces), drained
    8 stuffed green olives, sliced
    4 thin slices of sweet onion
    4 fresh dill or parsley sprigs
    4 paper-thin lemon slices

Cut crusts from bread. Spread 1 teaspoon butter on each slice of bread, covering completely. Arrange one-fourth of sardines and one-fourth of olives on each piece of bread. Top each with an onion slice. Garnish each with dill or parsley and lemon. Makes 4 sandwiches.

Smoked Salmon Smørrebrød

Laks—Denmark

Use the thin slicing blade of your food processor to cut paper-thin slices of cucumber.

    4 slices Danish Pumpernickel (page 247) or French bread
    4 teaspoons butter, softened
    1 package cream cheese (3 ounces), softened
    4 butter or leaf lettuce leaves
    ¼ pound smoked salmon, trout, herring, or whitefish
    1 European-style cucumber or other cucumber (5 inches), sliced paper thin
    4 paper-thin lemon slices, if desired

Cut crusts from pumpernickel, but not from French bread. Spread 1 teaspoon butter on each slice of bread, covering completely. Spread each with cream cheese. Gather lettuce leaves in ruffles. Place each ruffled leaf on 1 end of a slice of bread. Press into cream cheese to hold in place. Flake fish; arrange one-fourth on each sandwich, in an even layer. Gather several cucumber slices in your fingers, ruffling them together. Pile on top of fish. Garnish with a lemon slice. Makes 4 sandwiches.

Turkey-Lingonberry Smørrebrød
Kalkun—Denmark

Purchase cooked, thinly sliced turkey from a delicatessen.

> 4 teaspoons butter, softened
> 4 slices French bread
> 2 teaspoons Dijon mustard
> 4 small butter or leaf lettuce leaves
> 4 paper-thin slices cold cooked turkey breast
> ¼ cup fresh whole lingonberries or cooked whole cranberries

Spread 1 teaspoon butter on each slice of bread, covering completely. Spread each with ½ teaspoon mustard. Gather lettuce leaves into ruffles; place 1 ruffled leaf on 1 end of each buttered bread. Top each with a slice of turkey breast, letting some of lettuce extend beyond turkey. Garnish with lingonberries or cranberries. Makes 4 sandwiches.

Ham and Egg Smørrebrød

Skinke med Æg—Denmark

Ham and vegetables make this smørrebrød as colorful as a garden of flowers.

6 slices whole-wheat bread
7 teaspoons butter, softened
1 egg, thoroughly beaten
6 thin, cooked ham slices
12 paper-thin cucumber slices
6 tomato slices
6 butter or leaf lettuce leaves
Parsley or watercress

Cut crusts from bread. Spread 1 teaspoon butter on each slice of bread, covering completely; set aside. Over low heat, melt remaining teaspoon butter in a skillet or omelet pan that measures 8 inches across bottom. Add beaten egg; swirl pan until egg covers bottom of pan. Cook only until egg is set and surface feels dry. Cut into ½-inch strips; let cool. Roll ham slices into cones. Gather lettuce leaves in ruffles. Place each ruffled leaf on 1 end of each slice of buttered bread. Place 1 ham cone on part of each slice not covered with lettuce. Loosely roll up cooled egg strips. Place 1 rolled egg strip inside wide end of each ham cone. Cut each cucumber and tomato slice from center to outer edge, cutting through peel. Twist cucumber slices and tomato slices and place on top of ham. Garnish with parsley or watercress. Makes 6 sandwiches.

Cheese and Grape Smørrebrød

Danablu med Frugt—Denmark

This can serve as an excellent dessert smørrebrød for those who don't want sweets.

    4 thin slices firm white or French bread
    4 teaspoons butter, softened
    4 slices Danish blue, Mycella, or other blue cheese (4 ounces)
    4 small bunches seedless green grapes

Cut crusts from white bread, but not from French bread. Spread 1 teaspoon butter on each slice of bread, covering completely. Top each with a slice of blue cheese. If bread shows beneath cheese, cut off excess bread or spread cheese to cover. Press 1 bunch of grapes into blue cheese on each sandwich. Makes 4 dessert sandwiches.

Cheese and Strawberry Smørrebrød

Flødeost med Jordbær—Denmark

A marvelous combination of flavors!

    4 thin slices firm white or French bread
    4 teaspoons butter, softened
    1 package cream cheese (3 ounces), cut in 4 slices
    4 crisp green pepper rings
    8 large strawberries, hulled, halved

Cut crusts from white bread, but not from French bread. Spread 1 teaspoon butter on each slice of bread, covering completely. Top each with a slice of cream cheese. Spread cheese, covering bread. Top each with a green pepper ring and 4 strawberries halves. Makes 4 dessert sandwiches.

Havarti and Walnut Smørrebrød

Havarti med Nødder—Denmark

Use any aged cheese for this dessert smørrebrød.

    4 slices firm white or French bread
    4 teaspoons butter, softened
    4 to 8 slices aged Havarti or other strongly flavored cheese (4 to 6 ounces)
    16 walnut halves
    About 3 tablespoons orange marmalade

Cut crusts from white bread, but not from French bread. Spread 1 teaspoon butter on each slice of bread, covering completely. Top each slice with enough cheese to cover bread completely and one walnut half. Spoon a small dollop of orange marmalade on top of each walnut. Makes 4 dessert sandwiches.

❀Lunches and Suppers

Winter Fun Party

MENU

Potato Flatbread

Rye and Wheat Flatbread

Pea Soup with Pork

Rye-Meal Bread (page 246), Cheese

Sliced Tomatoes and Butter Lettuce

Apple Pie, Whipped Cream

Fruit-Juice Glögg (page 159)

Beer Punch

SCANDINAVIANS ARE AVID OUTDOOR SPORTS FANS—never mind the cold winter weather. By February, the days have become longer, though not much warmer. With more daylight hours, people spend time outside, enjoying ice skating and cross-country skiing.

Physical fitness and competition are historically important to Scandinavians, dating back to the Vikings with their superb physical stamina. Annual marathons and races, such as the *Finlandia* ski race, Sweden's Vasaloppet cross-country ski race, and the Norwegian Birkebeiner race, have inspired similar competitions worldwide.

But outdoor activities are not limited to professional sportsmen and women. In Denmark, laborers, business people, parents, and school children skate wherever there is ice. Some have lakes and ponds available to them. In the towns, tennis courts and football and soccer fields are flooded to make ice for skating.

Cross-country skiing takes the prize for popularity as a winter sport. As often as they can, Norwegians head for their huts in the mountains for weekends of ski touring. In Sweden and Finland, people take airplanes or trains to the snow-covered slopes of Lapland to enjoy ski holidays and weekends.

If you travel to Finland or Sweden, there are several Lapland resorts where you can stay and enjoy days of cross-country skiing on the sloping *fells* or mountains. In Finland, you can stay in rustic holiday-village log cabins with fully equipped kitchens. Or you may prefer a country farmhouse on a full-board basis. Accommodations may be simple, but they are immaculate. Meals are enjoyed with the family. Wherever you stay, you'll experience exhilarating sauna baths.

This menu is meant to warm you after a day on the slopes. It can be easily prepared in the simple kitchen of a vacation home or in your own home.

Potato Flatbread

Lefse—Norway

Norwegians serve lefse for all special occasions, including a coffeetable (page 265).

> 2½ pounds (5 to 6 large) russet potatoes, pared and quartered
> ½ cup (1 stick) butter
> ½ cup whipping cream
> 2 teaspoons sugar
> 1¼ teaspoons salt
> 1½ cups all-purpose flour

In a medium saucepan over medium heat, cook potatoes in water to cover until they are just tender, not mushy, about 20 minutes. Pour into a colander over a bowl and drain well. (When the steam rises from the potatoes, you will see a floury-white exterior on the potato pieces.) I save the potato water for making bread or use it in soup.

Press the dry, hot potatoes through a potato ricer into a large bowl. Mix in the butter, whipping cream, sugar, and salt with a potato masher until very well blended. Note that the flour is *not* added now! Smooth the mixture out in the bowl.

Refrigerate (do *not* cover) at least eight hours or overnight; this is so that the potato mixture will dry out as it chills.

The next day, preheat an ungreased flat grill to 450°F. Place a clean, large terry towel on a large plastic bag. You will place the baked lefse on one end of the towel and fold the other half of the towel and the plastic bag over the lefse as you cook more rounds. The towel will absorb moisture from the lefse as it cools, and the plastic keeps the moisture in the towel.

For rolling out the lefse, stretch a pastry cloth over a board and use tape to fasten it so it is taut. Cover a regular or grooved lefse rolling pin with a pastry sock and rub flour generously into the sock.

Remove bowl with potato mixture from refrigerator. Wash your hands well. Add the flour and work it in using your hands. Once the flour is added, you *must* roll out and cook all of the lefse or the dough will get soft and sticky.

Using a #13 ice-cream scoop (measures ⅓ cup), portion out the potato mixture and shape into balls. Smooth out the balls and dust lightly with additional flour.

Generously flour the pastry cloth and the rolling pin as well. Flatten all of the dough and begin rolling it out as thin as you can, adding more flour as you go, being careful not to let the dough stick to the pin or the pastry board. Keep everything dry! Loosen the lefse often using a lefse stick, carefully pushing it between the dough and the board.

When the round is as large and thin as you can make it, use the stick to pick up the round and transfer it to the hot (ungreased) lefse griddle. The griddle should be hot enough that the lefse immediately begins to bubble. When a peek at the grilled side shows a nice surface of brown spots, slide the stick under it and carefully flip it over. The stick must be dry so that the lefse will not stick to it and tear.

If the edges of the lefse begin to get dry, brown, and curl, you are cooking the rounds too long, and if the lefse is not browning well, but remaining light, the griddle temperature is set too low. If the lefse quickly burns, the griddle temperature is too high. Because all griddles vary a little in their temperature, it takes a little bit of practice to get it exactly right. Place the cooked lefse onto one end of the terry towel and cover with the other half of the towel, covering at the same time with the other half of the large plastic bag.

Continue rolling out rounds and cooking them, stacking them right on top of each other in the terry towel (there is no need to separate them).

Allow the stack of lefse to cool 2–3 hours, then carefully peel each round off the pile, fold it into quarters, and stack them in zipper-lock freezer bags. I like to put 6 to 12 in each bag, depending on how many I think we'll be using at a time. Refrigerate the lefse that will be eaten within the next three days. Freeze the rest.

Lefse is delicious spread with butter and sprinkled with a little white or brown sugar, or sugar and cinnamon. Some people roll up the sugared lefse tightly and then slice it into ½-inch slices and serve right along with cookies on the holiday cookie tray. Lefse is also delicious just buttered and served with a holiday dinner.

Makes about 20 rounds.

Rye and Wheat Flatbread
Flatbrød—Scandinavia

Serve these oven-baked crackers with cheese or other spreads.

1½ cups boiling water
2 tablespoons butter
½ teaspoon salt
1 cup stirred rye flour
1 cup all-purpose flour
1 cup whole-wheat flour

Preheat oven to 450°F (230°C). In a large bowl, combine water, butter, salt, rye flour, and all-purpose flour. Beat well. Stir in whole-wheat flour until dough is smooth and resembles baking powder biscuit dough. Divide dough into 4 portions. Cut each portion into quarters. On a generously floured board, roll out each piece of dough to make a thin 10- to 12-inch circle. If desired, use a hardtack or lefse rolling pin (page xv, xvi) to make a pattern on dough. Place 2 or 3 dough circles on an ungreased baking sheet. Bake in preheated oven 3 to 5 minutes or until crisp but not completely browned. Cool baked breads on a rack. Stack 6 completely cooled breads together; wrap airtight. Store in a cool dry place. To serve, break into pieces. Makes 16 breads.

Pea Soup with Pork

Ärter med Fläsk—Sweden

After a frolic in the cold winter air, this is the perfect soup to serve—with pork sandwiches.

2 cups dried yellow Swedish peas
3 quarts water
1 fresh pork shoulder roast (2 to 3 pounds)
3 medium onions, sliced
½ teaspoon ground ginger
¼ teaspoon whole allspice
1 teaspoon dried leaf marjoram
1 teaspoon salt or to taste
⅛ teaspoon ground black pepper

Sort and wash peas. In a deep soup kettle, combine peas and water. Soak overnight. Place soup kettle with soaked peas and water over medium-high heat. Bring to a boil. Remove shells of peas that float to top of water. Simmer 2 hours or until peas are partially softened. Add pork roast, onions, ginger, and allspice. Simmer 2 to 3 hours until pork is tender. Skim fat from surface. Stir in marjoram, salt, and pepper. To serve, place pork roast on a platter; cut into slices, removing bone. Serve pork in sandwiches, if desired. Serve hot soup in bowls or mugs. Makes 6 servings.

Apple Pie

Eplepai—Norway

For a real treat, serve this fresh from the oven, topped with a dollop of whipped cream.

> 1 egg
> ¾ cup sugar
> 1 teaspoon vanilla extract
> 1 teaspoon baking powder
> ¼ teaspoon salt
> 1 teaspoon ground cinnamon
> ½ cup all-purpose flour
> ½ cup chopped pecans or walnuts
> 2 small, tart apples, diced (about 1 cup)
> Whipped cream or cinnamon ice cream

Generously butter a 9-inch pie pan; set aside. Preheat oven to 350°F (175°C). In a large bowl, combine all ingredients except whipped cream or ice cream. Stir until blended; mixture will be stiff. Spoon into prepared pie pan. Bake 30 minutes or until browned and slightly puffed. To serve, cut hot pie into wedges; top with dollops of whipped cream or ice cream. Makes 6 to 8 servings.

Beer Punch

Mumma—Sweden

This is exceptionally good when you use Scandinavian or German beer.

1 bottle dark beer (12 ounces)
1 bottle light beer (12 ounces)
1 bottle pale ale (12 ounces)
¼ cup aquavit or gin

Refrigerate all ingredients until chilled. To serve, pour all ingredients into a chilled pitcher; stir. Serve in mugs. Makes 6 servings.

Supper at Grandma's Farm

MENU

Grandma Norland's Meat Loaf

Summer House Pork Chops

Cabbage Rolls

Potato Dumplings, Apple Slaw

Carrot Casserole (page 215)

Caramel Pudding

Milk, Buttermilk, Coffee, Tea

DOWN-HOME SCANDINAVIAN COOKING is usually simple, hearty, and nutritious. The recipes in this menu illustrate techniques that Scandinavian cooks have learned and passed down for generations. For instance, a Norwegian grandmother has taught her daughters and granddaughters how to make the lightest-textured, tenderest meat loaf imaginable. The secret lies in beating the meat mixture vigorously—just as carefully as you beat the eggs for a sponge cake.

Norwegians are masters at long, slow simmering. This technique is used to make *Dravle* or Caramel Pudding. The milk is boiled gently until it becomes a slightly sweet, caramel-flavored concentrate. It is delicious with the addition of walnuts. However, nuts aren't traditional.

Famous Norwegian *gjetost* cheese is another example of long, slow simmering. In other countries, the *whey,* or fluid left after making cheese, is usually fed to cattle. In Norway, it is cooked down until it forms a caramel-flavored thick paste, which cools to a solid, tan cheese. *Ekte gjetost* is made with 100 percent goat's-milk whey. It is in much smaller supply than regular gjetost, a mixture of 10 percent goat's-milk whey and 90 percent cow's-milk whey.

Another Norwegian cheese, *gammelost,* or *old cheese,* is made from skim milk. Old-timers insist they owe their present good health and strength to gammelost. It is low in calories and fat and very high in protein—and very aromatic. To eat gammelost, generously spread butter over a piece of dark bread, then top with a thin shaving of gammelost. Nibble slowly.

Recipes are handed down from generation to generation with slight variations as the spirit and available ingredients dictate. The recipe for Potato Dumplings, rich with hearty flavor, has been handed down for at least six generations in one Norwegian family.

From this menu, choose one of the main dishes to serve with the dumplings.

Grandma Norland's Meat Loaf

Kjøttpudding—Norway

This meatloaf makes excellent cold sandwiches.

2 pounds lean ground beef
1 pound lean ground pork
1 cup milk
1 tablespoon all-purpose flour
1 egg
1 small onion, minced
2½ teaspoons salt
½ teaspoon pepper
½ teaspoon ground allspice

Butter a 9 x 5-inch loaf pan; set aside. Preheat oven to 325°F (165°C). In large bowl of electric mixer, combine beef, pork, milk, flour, and egg. Beat at low speed until blended, then on high speed 10 minutes or until light and fluffy. Using a wooden spoon, stir in onion, salt, pepper, and allspice. Spoon mixture into prepared pan. Bake 1½ hours or until loaf shrinks away from sides of pan. Makes 8 servings.

Summer House Pork Chops
Sommer Koteletter—Denmark

The combined aromas and flavors of apples, onions, and curry powder here are wonderful.

    1 tablespoon butter
    4 pork loin chops, 1 inch thick
    3 tart apples, peeled, cored, sliced
    1 large onion, diced
    1 teaspoon salt
    1 teaspoon sugar
    ¼ teaspoon black pepper
    1 teaspoon curry powder
    1 tablespoon butter, melted
    ⅓ cup dry breadcrumbs

Preheat oven to 350°F (175°C). Melt 1 tablespoon butter in a large oven-proof skillet over medium heat. Brown pork chops in butter, 3 to 5 minutes on each side. Remove pork chops from skillet. Add apples, onion, salt, sugar, pepper, and curry powder to skillet. Arrange browned chops over apple layer. Cover and bake 30 minutes or until chops are tender and apple layer is cooked through. In a small bowl, stir melted butter into breadcrumbs. Sprinkle over baked pork chops. Bake, uncovered, 5 to 10 minutes longer or until crumbs are crisp and browned. Makes 4 servings.

Cabbage Rolls

Kåldomar—Scandinavian

A favorite in all of the Scandinavian countries.

2 to 3 quarts boiling water
1 large head cabbage
1 pound lean ground beef
1 pound lean ground pork
1½ cups soft breadcrumbs
1 small onion, minced
1 egg
2 teaspoons salt
½ teaspoon ground allspice
1 cup milk
2 tablespoons butter, melted
½ cup whipping cream

Preheat oven to 300°F (150°C). Butter a 13 x 9-inch baking pan; set aside. Remove 16 unblemished large outer leaves from cabbage. Cook leaves in boiling water 1 minute or until softened. Or, place head of cabbage in water. After 1 minute, drain. Remove 16 outer leaves from cabbage. Reserve remaining cabbage for another use. Drain softened leaves on paper towels. In large bowl of electric mixer, combine beef, pork, breadcrumbs, onion, egg, salt, allspice, and milk. Beat with electric mixer on high speed until mixture is light and fluffy, about 10 minutes. Divide meat mixture among cabbage leaves, placing an egg-shaped mound near the stem end of each leaf. Roll into bundles, folding sides of cabbage leaves over meat mixture. Arrange cabbage rolls close together, in prepared baking pan, with loose end of leaf on bottom. Brush rolls with melted butter. Bake 1 hour. Drain juices from pan into a large skillet. Over high heat, bring juices to a rolling boil; boil until reduced to make a shiny glaze. Slowly stir cream into glaze. Bring to a boil again. Stirring occasionally, cook until thickened. Arrange cooked cabbage rolls in a shallow bowl. Pour sauce over cabbage rolls. Serve hot. Makes 8 servings or 16 cabbage rolls.

Potato Dumplings

Kumle—Norway

Every Norwegian cook has her own favorite version of potato dumplings.

> 4 cups shredded raw potatoes
> 2 cups all-purpose flour
> 1 tablespoon salt
> 8 to 12 cups beef, ham, or chicken broth
> 16 cubes (½ inch) cooked ham
> Melted butter
> Chopped parsley

Place potatoes in a strainer. Rinse with cold water to prevent browning; drain well. In a large bowl, combine flour and salt. Add drained potatoes; stir until potatoes are coated. In a deep medium saucepan, bring broth to a boil over medium heat. Using a serving spoon, scoop a rounded spoonful of potato mixture, about the size of a large egg. Press 1 cube of ham into center, covering completely. Using a slotted spoon, carefully lower dumpling into hot broth. Quickly shape remaining dumplings with ham cubes in center and lower into hot broth. Adjust heat to maintain a simmer but not a hard boil. Simmer at least 45 minutes, turning dumplings over after about 25 minutes. Use a slotted spoon to lift cooked dumplings from hot broth. Serve hot dumplings as a vegetable dish with melted butter. Garnish with chopped parsley. Or serve with broth, or in broth as a soup. Makes about 16 dumplings or 6 to 8 servings.

Apple Slaw

Æblesalat—Denmark

Slaw with fruit in it is a Scandinavian favorite.

½ cup whipping cream
½ cup mayonnaise
1 tablespoon sugar
1 large Red Delicious or Winesap apple
4 cups finely shredded cabbage
1 can crushed pineapple (8 ounces), drained

In a large bowl, combine cream, mayonnaise, and sugar. Core apple; dice but do not peel. Add diced apple and cabbage to mayonnaise mixture. Fold in pineapple. Refrigerate until ready to serve. Makes 8 servings.

Caramel Pudding

Dravle—Norway

Milk-sugar caramelizes during long slow cooking to flavor this dessert.

½ gallon homogenized whole milk
2 eggs, slightly beaten
1 cup dairy sour cream
1 tablespoon all-purpose flour
½ cup sugar
½ cup chopped walnuts

Pour milk into a heavy 4-quart saucepan. Stirring constantly, bring to a boil over medium-low heat. Reduce heat to lowest possible setting. Stirring occasionally, simmer 3 to 4 hours or until milk is reduced to about 4 cups and has a light tan color. In a small bowl, blend eggs, sour cream, flour, and sugar. Stir ½ cup hot milk into egg mixture. Stir egg mixture into remaining hot milk. Cook and stir over low heat until mixture is thickened and slightly curdled, about 10 minutes. Serve hot, sprinkled with walnuts. Makes 8 servings.

❁Holidays

Easter Festival

MENU

Caviar and Potato Slices

Crown Roast of Pork Piquant

Bergen Easter Chicken

Tomato Salad

Glazed Mushrooms

Brussels Sprouts

Finnish Cheesecake

Schnapps, Beer, Milk, Buttermilk, Coffee

Red Currant Juice, White or Red Wine

EASTER IN SCANDINAVIA is a festival of sun, snow, and skiing. Norwegians head for the mountains and observe Easter in a mountain *hytta*, or private hideaway, spending as many hours as possible ski-touring long distances. Finns, Swedes, and Danes take the long weekend to head for snowy slopes, if not to Lapland, then to other places in Europe.

Before Easter, the open markets across Scandinavia are filled with arrangements of brilliantly colored chicken feathers tied to leafy birch twigs. The birch twigs are clipped from branches two to three weeks earlier and placed in water to force the green leaves to open. Leafy branches are used to decorate homes. The weather is still cold and there are no flowers blooming, so the dyed chicken feathers make a colorful substitute.

On an Easter visit to relatives in Western Finland, we saw Easter Saturday bonfires in the field across from the house, set to scare away "witches." Answering a knock on the door, we found two little girls, faces blackened with soot, dressed in witch costumes. Each carried a broomstick with a copper coffeepot hung on the end. Witches, of course, love hot black coffee. Our Great Aunt Lilja stuffed chocolates and Easter eggs into the pots. Then, the little "witches" flew off to the neighbors. We spent the evening witnessing a procession of witches and other scary creatures—despite bonfires!

Although there are no traditional Scandinavian Easter foods, there are regional favorites. Swedes and Norwegians always include fish on the menu. Norwegians like chicken as a main course, even though it is quite expensive in Scandinavia. In all countries, pork and lamb dishes are popular.

Finland has a traditional dessert called *mämmi*. This almost black pudding is made of rye, malt, and molasses, and is baked in a birchbark basket. Mämmi is a food for which one must acquire a taste. Eastern Finland celebrates Easter with a cheesecake-like dessert called *Pasha*. It is generally served alone, but we suggest a wonderful musk-flavored cloudberry sauce. Scandinavian specialty shops often carry cloudberry preserves.

Caviar and Potato Slices

Kaviar med Kartoffler—Denmark

This is one of the simplest and most impressive hors d'oeuvres!

½ cup vegetable oil
4 medium potatoes
½ cup dairy sour cream
1 jar red or black caviar (2 ounces)

Preheat oven to 500°F (260°C). Spread ¼ cup oil in each of 2 jelly-roll pans. Scrub potatoes thoroughly. Cut potatoes crosswise into ¼-inch slices; rinse under very cold water to prevent browning. Dry on paper towels. Dip both sides of potato slices in oil in prepared pans, then arrange in pans in a single layer. Bake 10 to 12 minutes or until potatoes are crisp around edges and lightly browned. Drain on paper towels, if desired. Arrange baked potato slices on a platter or tray. Top each with a dollop of sour cream and about ¼ teaspoon caviar. Serve immediately. Makes about 32 appetizers.

Crown Roast of Pork Piquant
Svinekam—Denmark

The mustard glaze gives this pork roast a special flavor.

½ cup Dijon mustard
2 tablespoons grated fresh horseradish
2 teaspoons anchovy paste
2 tablespoons brown sugar
1 crown roast of pork (16 ribs, 8 pounds)
1 cup fine dry breadcrumbs

Preheat oven to 325°F (165°C). In a small bowl, combine mustard, horse-radish, anchovy paste, and brown sugar. Place pork roast on a rack in a large roasting pan. Place an inverted metal measuring cup, empty can, or glass in center of roast to maintain shape. Brush mustard mixture on all sides of meat. Coat evenly with breadcrumbs. Insert meat thermometer into thickest part of roast, not touching bone. Bake until thermometer registers 180°F (80°C), 35 to 40 minutes per pound. Let stand 20 minutes before carving. Remove cup, can, or glass from center. Carve roast and serve on a round platter. Makes 16 servings.

Bergen Easter Chicken

Stekt Påske Kylling—Norway

Gjetost, the caramel-colored whey cheese of Norway, adds color and richness to the sauce.

1 broiler-fryer chicken, cut up (3 pounds)
1 teaspoon salt
½ teaspoon ground white pepper
2 tablespoons butter
1 cup chicken broth or water
¼ cup sherry or 2 tablespoons lemon juice
¼ cup chopped fresh parsley
½ cup whipping cream
1 cup shredded gjetost or aged Cheddar cheese (4 ounces)
Chopped fresh parsley for garnish

Remove skin from chicken; rub meat with salt and pepper. Melt butter in a large skillet over medium heat. Add chicken; brown on all sides. Pour broth or water over browned chicken. Add sherry or lemon juice. Cover; reduce heat to low. Simmer 35 to 45 minutes or until chicken is tender. Use a slotted spoon to place cooked chicken on a platter; keep warm. Add ¼ cup chopped parsley and cream to drippings in pan. Stirring constantly, bring to a simmer. Cook and stir until sauce is reduced to about 1 cup and has a glazed appearance. Stir in cheese only until melted. Pour sauce over chicken. Garnish with fresh parsley. Makes 4 servings.

Tomato Salad

Tomatisallad—Sweden

Tomatoes and cucumbers are popular in Sweden.

6 medium tomatoes
Boiling water
4 green onions with tops, sliced
2 tablespoons red or white wine vinegar
1 tablespoon sugar
½ teaspoon crushed whole allspice
¼ teaspoon ground white pepper
2 teaspoons salt
¼ cup vegetable oil
1 European-style or other cucumber (8 inches), sliced paper-thin
Chopped fresh parsley for garnish

Immerse tomatoes in boiling water, about 15 seconds. Immerse in cold water, then quickly core and peel. Cut peeled tomatoes into thin slices; arrange in a 2-inch-deep platter. Sprinkle with green onions. In a small bowl, whisk together vinegar, sugar, allspice, white pepper, and 1 teaspoon salt. Slowly whisk in oil until blended. Pour over tomatoes. Drain cucumbers on paper towels; sprinkle with remaining teaspoon salt. Pat dry with paper towels. Loosely pile cucumbers in a mound on center of platter over tomato slices. Sprinkle with parsley. Serve immediately or refrigerate up to 6 hours before serving. Makes 8 to 10 servings.

Glazed Mushrooms

Glaserede Champignon—Denmark

Danes are known for marvelous combinations such as this one.

1 pound whole small mushrooms
¼ cup olive oil or vegetable oil
½ teaspoon salt
½ teaspoon paprika
1 garlic clove, crushed
1 small green onion, chopped
3 tablespoons chopped parsley
1 tablespoon chopped fresh dill, if desired
2 teaspoons dried leaf basil

Clean mushrooms. Remove stems; reserve for another use. Heat oil in a large skillet over medium heat. Stir in salt, paprika, garlic, and green onion. Increase heat to high. Add mushrooms; sauté until mushrooms are glazed and coated with oil mixture, 3 to 5 minutes. Top with parsley, dill, if desired, and basil; toss lightly. Serve immediately. Makes 8 servings.

Finnish Cheesecake

Pasha—Finland

Traditionally, this is served plain, but we prefer the variation given below.

2 quarts dairy buttermilk
1 egg
1 cup dairy sour cream
½ cup sugar
½ cup ground almonds
½ cup butter
½ teaspoon vanilla extract

Pour buttermilk into a 3-quart casserole dish. Cover and place in oven. Begin heating oven to 250°F (120°C). Also begin timing; bake 3 hours. Line a large strainer with several layers of cheesecloth or paper towels. Place lined strainer over a large, deep bowl. Pour mixture into lined strainer; let drain overnight. Discard whey or save for another use. Pour curd from lined strainer into a large bowl. Beat in egg, then sour cream, sugar, and almonds. Melt butter in a heavy, large saucepan. Stir curd mixture into melted butter. Attach a candy thermometer to side of pan with bulb in curd mixture. Stir mixture over medium heat until thermometer reaches 190°F to 200°F (90°C to 95°C). Do not scorch. Stir in vanilla. Line a wooden cheese mold or an unglazed clay flowerpot with a double thickness of cheesecloth. Place mold in a medium bowl. Spoon mixture into mold; fold edges of cheesecloth over top of curd mixture. Press down to compact mixture. Place a small plate or saucer on top of mixture, then place a weight on top. Refrigerate 2 to 3 days. Remove mold from bowl; pull back folded cheesecloth. Invert mold onto a plate. Remove mold and cheesecloth. To serve, cut into ½-inch horizontal slices. Makes 8 servings.

Variation

Blend 1 cup cloudberry or raspberry preserves with ¼ cup orange juice or orange-flavored liqueur. Spoon a small amount onto each plate, then top with a slice of Finnish Cheesecake.

Christmas Eve Supper

MENU

Christmas Cod, White Sauce

Swedish Meatballs

Dilled Green Peas, Boiled Potatoes

Potato Flatbread (page 45)

Finnish Rice Pudding

Milk, Coffee, Fruit-Juice Glögg (page 159)

IN SWEDEN, SANTA CLAUS is a *Tomte,* or gnome—a tiny little fellow who lives somewhere among the outbuildings. Father or an uncle or neighbor dresses up as the Christmas Tomte to hand out gifts. He is a bit on the large side, but the children don't seem to notice.

In Denmark, they begin celebrating Christmas on the first day of December. *Julenisse,* the Danish counterpart of the Swedish Tomte, delivers a gift to the children every day for twenty-three days!

In Scandinavia, the Christmas tree is never in place until Christmas Eve. In Denmark, this is a dramatic affair. Adults decorate the tree with handmade ornaments—angels, birds, apples, hearts, cookies—and real candles. The children are not allowed to see the tree until the candles are lit. As they enter the room with the youngest child leading the way, everyone joins hands and circles the tree, singing Christmas carols. They sing at least ten Christmas carols, then open gifts.

In Norway, church bells begin ringing at 4:00 P.M. on Christmas Eve. The bells are a signal that Christmas is beginning. After church, the children go on a *julebukke* round, visiting the homes of relatives and friends where they are treated to Christmas cookies and other goodies. At home, the tree is being trimmed, and the mysterious little Julenisse makes his way down each chimney and delivers gifts.

When the children arrive at home, the family has a light supper or a full smörgåsbord. After supper, the family sings and dances around the Christmas tree. The lucky person who got an almond in his or her rice pudding is usually named the Julenisse for the evening and gets to distribute the gifts.

Christmas traditions vary among families. For many, Christmas Eve is the time for a big, traditional dinner or smörgåsbord. For others, supper may simply be rice pudding—nothing else. Or it may be *lutefisk,* meatballs, and rice pudding. Meatballs are always served as an alternative for those who do not like lutefisk.

In Finland, large pots of tar are burned on either side of the entrance to the church to commemorate those who lost their lives in wars for independence. Candles are lit and placed on graves throughout the cemetery that surrounds the church. On Christmas Eve, the night is black and snow covers the ground in deep drifts, making the scene one of awe and beauty.

After supper, *Joulupukki,* or Santa Claus, warmly dressed in a long red coat, pointed leather boots, a warm red wool cap, and thick mittens, knocks at the door. He asks the children if they have been good and to prove it by singing a song. The children, wearing red pointed *tonttu,* or gnome hats, nervously but obediently sing. Joulupukki praises them profusely, then distributes gifts.

Christmas Cod

Lutefisk—Sweden

Ready-to-cook lutefisk can be purchased in specialty stores, gourmet stores, and supermarkets.

> 4 pounds lutefisk or cod
> Boiling water
> 1 teaspoon salt
> ¼ teaspoon ground white pepper
> ¼ teaspoon ground allspice
> ½ cup butter, melted
> White Sauce (page 73)

Remove skin from fish. Bones are large enough to remove easily after fish is served. Place fish in a deep pot; cover with boiling water. Bring to a simmer over medium-low heat; do not boil. Simmer 10 to 15 minutes or until fish flakes easily, quivers like jelly, and becomes translucent. Drain fish; place on a hot platter. Sprinkle with salt, white pepper, and allspice. Drizzle melted butter over fish. Serve with White Sauce. Makes 4 to 6 servings.

White Sauce
Vit Sås—Sweden

The secret to a smooth sauce is to stir constantly.

¼ cup butter
¼ cup all-purpose flour
1½ cups milk
1 teaspoon salt
¼ teaspoon ground allspice or white pepper

Melt butter in a medium saucepan over medium heat. Stir in flour. Slowly stir in milk. Stirring constantly, cook until sauce is thickened and smooth. Stir in salt and allspice or white pepper. Serve hot. Makes about 2 cups.

Swedish Meatballs

Köttbullar—Sweden

Serve meatballs as an alternative main dish for those who don't care for lutefisk.

1½ cups soft breadcrumbs
1 cup half-and-half
1 tablespoon butter
½ cup chopped onion
1 pound lean ground beef
½ pound lean ground pork
1 egg
¼ cup minced fresh parsley
1½ teaspoons salt
½ teaspoon ground ginger
½ teaspoon ground allspice
½ teaspoon ground nutmeg
2 tablespoons butter
2 tablespoons all-purpose flour
2 cups beef broth

In large bowl of electric mixer, soak breadcrumbs in half-and-half for 10 minutes. Melt 1 tablespoon butter in a large skillet over medium heat. Add onion; sauté until soft, about 3 minutes. Stir into breadcrumb mixture. Add beef, pork, egg, parsley, salt, ginger, allspice, and nutmeg. With electric mixer, beat at high speed until mixture is fluffy. Dip 2 teaspoons in ice water until cold. Use cold spoons to shape meat mixture into tiny meatballs. Melt 2 tablespoons butter in skillet used to sauté onion. Brown meatballs in butter, turning to brown evenly on all sides. Drain cooked meatballs on paper towels. Stir flour into drippings in skillet. Gradually whisk in broth. Continue stirring until mixture thickens. Return meatballs to sauce in skillet. Simmer 15 minutes or until meatballs are heated through. Makes 4 to 6 servings or about 48 meatballs.

Dilled Green Peas

Tilliherneet—Finland

Green peas, seasoned with dill and topped with cheese—absolutely delicious!

2 packages frozen green peas (10 ounces each)
2 tablespoons butter
2 tablespoons chopped shallots or green onions
1 teaspoon dried dill weed
2 tablespoons chopped pimiento
1 cup shredded Jarlsberg cheese (4 ounces)

Cook peas as package directs. Melt butter in a small skillet over medium heat. Add shallots or green onions; sauté 2 minutes or until soft. Stir in hot cooked peas, dill, and pimiento. Pour into a serving dish; sprinkle cheese over top. Serve immediately. Makes 6 servings.

Finnish Rice Pudding

Riisipuuro—Finland

All Scandinavian countries claim this creamy rice pudding as their own.

½ cup sugar
1 tablespoon ground cinnamon
¾ cup medium-grain rice, uncooked
¾ cup water
2 tablespoons butter
4 cups milk
1 teaspoon salt
1 cinnamon stick (3 inches)
¼ teaspoon ground nutmeg
1 teaspoon grated lemon peel
1 teaspoon vanilla extract
1 whole almond, shelled, blanched
About ¼ cup butter, melted

In a small bowl, combine sugar and ground cinnamon; set aside. In a large saucepan, combine rice and water. Bring to boil over medium-high heat. Stir in 2 tablespoons butter, milk, salt, and cinnamon stick. Simmer over low heat, uncovered, stirring occasionally until thickened, about 35 minutes. Remove cinnamon stick; stir in nutmeg, lemon peel, and vanilla. To serve, stir almond into pudding, then spoon into individual dessert dishes. Top each serving with cinnamon-sugar and melted butter. Serve hot. Makes 6 servings.

Old-Fashioned Christmas Smörgåsbord

Fruit-Juice Glögg (page 159)

Hot Wine Punch (page 203), Beer, Milk

———————

IN OLD SCANDINAVIA, feverish preparations for Christmas began early in December. Pressed-meat dishes had to be prepared and preserved, but were not tasted until Christmas Eve or Christmas Day. Most important was the home-preserved ham. Its preparation began during the first week of Advent, after the slaughtering of the *house pig*.

In the old days, every household had a special pig that was fed all the best table scraps throughout the year. It was named the *talous porsus* in Finland. Today, a family member who willingly cleans up the last bits of a meal may lovingly be called the talous porsus. As could be expected, the house pig became a family pet. It was difficult to face the slaughtering, much less the eating, of a pet, so families often exchanged animals.

The best ham was selected for the Christmas meal. It was brined, then smoked, if the farm had a smoke sauna. After two weeks of curing, the ham was baked in a rye crust. The good, rich broth in the baking pan tempted the family into the kitchen at about 2:00 P.M. on Christmas Eve to take part in a yearly ritual called *dip-in-the-kettle* or *doppa i grytan*. Everyone dipped a piece of bread, or the rye crust in which the ham was baked, into the steaming broth. After the crust was removed from the ham, the ham was coated with a mustard-crumb-sugar mixture and browned in preparation for the big meal.

In our menu, we have made the dip-in-the kettle custom the first-course serving of soup and bread. Serve the soup in bowls at the table or in mugs as a stand-up course. If you have a kitchen ceremony, as in olden days, let family members dip slices of buttered rye bread into the broth. Then, on a plate, serve a slice of the ham or some Christmas sausages. This little snack probably took the place of a midday meal on Christmas Eve because of the large evening smörgåsbord to follow.

To Swedish families, the aroma of the *Jul* ham baking the night before Christmas Eve is as important as the remaining holiday festivities. The traditional ham is large enough to last the entire holiday and is enjoyed for sandwiches and snacking after the main Christmas meal has been served.

Pickled herring, in many varieties, is always part of a smörgåsbord. Pickled herring is available in Scandinavian specialty shops or by mail. The recipe for Marinated Anchovies calls for Swedish anchovies as the main ingredient. Don't confuse *Swedish* anchovies with more salty *Portuguese* anchovies.

Let guests serve themselves from this smörgåsbord. First, serve Dip-in-the-Kettle Soup, then offer the herring dishes. For the third course, provide clean plates for the cold-meat dishes that were prepared weeks before Christmas. The main course, Home-Cured Christmas Ham, requires another clean dish. Serve a salad or a choice of salads. Boiled potatoes are always included. For dessert, give guests another clean plate and serve a variety of puddings or other desserts. Serve any or all of the selections buffet-style.

Many families serve a meal similar to this one on Christmas Day, and on Christmas Eve have a simple supper of Christmas Cod (page 72).

Dip-in-the-Kettle Soup

Doppa i Grytan—Sweden

Serve this thin, savory soup as a first course for Christmas dinner.

    6 cups ham or roast beef broth or canned broth
    Salt and pepper to taste
    Rye Dipping Bread (page 245), torn in pieces
    2 tablespoons butter, melted
    3 or 4 thin lemon slices

Pour broth into a large saucepan. Add salt and pepper to taste. Bring to a boil over medium heat. Toast bread in broiler. Sprinkle with butter. Pour hot broth into a soup tureen. Garnish with lemon slices. To serve, place pieces of toasted bread in 6 individual soup bowls. Pour broth over bread. Serve immediately. Makes 6 servings.

Marinated Anchovies

Marinerad Ansjovis—Sweden

Do not use Portuguese anchovies, which are smaller, saltier, and drier than Swedish anchovies.

1 can Swedish anchovy fillets (3 to 3½ ounces)
3 tablespoons vegetable oil
1 tablespoon white wine vinegar
⅛ teaspoon paprika
2 tablespoons thinly sliced green onion, with tops

Drain anchovies. Roll up fillets and arrange in rows in a small serving dish. In a small bowl, combine oil, vinegar, and paprika. Beat with a whisk. Pour over anchovies. Sprinkle with onion. Cover and refrigerate 2 or more hours. Baste occasionally to keep anchovies moist. Makes 12 or 13 marinated fillets.

Mustard Herring

Senapsill—Sweden

Purchase herring fillets in wine sauce from a specialty shop or supermarket, or online.

>1 jar of herring fillets in wine sauce (16 ounces)
>3 egg yolks
>1 tablespoon prepared Swedish- or German-style mustard
>1 tablespoon red wine vinegar
>½ teaspoon salt
>¼ teaspoon ground white pepper
>1 teaspoon sugar
>1 cup vegetable oil
>¼ cup dried dill weed, crumbled

Drain herring; place in a medium bowl. In a small bowl, combine egg yolks, mustard, vinegar, salt, white pepper, and sugar. Use a whisk to gradually beat in oil until mixture is thick and creamy. Stir in dill. Pour over herring. Cover and refrigerate 3 to 4 hours. Spoon into a serving bowl. Makes 12 to 16 herring pieces.

Pressed-Beef Roll
Rullepulse—Scandinavia

Start three days in advance to make this beef roll with a pork tenderloin center.

1½ pounds beef flank steak
1 teaspoon salt
1 teaspoon ground allspice
1 small onion, minced
1 pound whole pork tenderloin, fat removed
1 cup meat-curing salt, or 1 cup pickling salt and 2 tablespoons saltpeter
4 cups water
Cold water

Cut 2 pieces of plastic wrap twice as large as flank steak; set aside. Leaving 1 long edge not cut through, use a sharp knife to cut steak horizontally; or ask your butcher to *butterfly* the steak. Lay meat on 1 piece of plastic wrap, cut-side up. Top with second piece of plastic wrap. With flat side of a meat mallet or cleaver, pound meat until it is ⅓ to ½ inch thick. Remove and discard plastic wrap. Sprinkle flattened meat with 1 teaspoon salt, allspice, and onion. Place pork tenderloin on 1 end of meat, parallel to long grain of flank steak. Roll up meat tightly, jelly-roll fashion. Tie firmly with cotton string or, using a darning needle, sew steak to keep it rolled. Place in a nonmetal, 9 x 5-inch loaf pan. Dissolve meat-curing salt or pickling salt and saltpeter in 4 cups water. Pour over rolled meat. Brine should cover meat. Cover and refrigerate 48 hours. Remove meat from brine; discard brine. Place meat in a deep pot. Add cold water until 4 inches above meat. Bring to a boil; simmer over low heat 3 hours or until meat is tender when pierced with a fork. Add more water, if necessary, to keep meat covered. Lift meat from water; place in nonmetal loaf pan. Add cooking liquid to cover. Cover loosely with plastic wrap. Place a plate or other weight on meat to keep it submerged in cooking liquid. Refrigerate until chilled, about 1 hour. Discard liquid. Meat roll may be wrapped airtight and frozen. Thaw in wrapper in refrigerator for best flavor. To serve, remove string and cut in ¼-inch slices. Makes about 30 slices.

Pressed-Pork Roll

Käärysyltty—Finland

Have the butcher "butterfly" a boneless pork loin for you.

    1 boneless pork loin (4 pounds)
    ½ teaspoon pepper
    Boiling water
    2 tablespoons salt
    ½ teaspoon ground ginger
    6 whole allspice
    1 onion, thinly sliced
    1 carrot, thinly sliced

Cut 2 pieces of plastic wrap, twice as large as meat. Lay pork loin on a flat surface. Use a sharp knife to cut meat horizontally, leaving 1 long edge not cut through. This is called *butterflying*. Meat will be about 1 inch thick. Lay meat, cut-side up, between pieces of plastic wrap. With flat side of a meat mallet or cleaver, pound meat until about ½ inch thick. Remove and discard plastic wrap. Sprinkle meat with pepper; roll up tightly, jelly-roll fashion, beginning on 1 long side. Tie with cotton string or, using a darning needle, sew meat to keep it rolled. Place rolled meat in a large, deep pot. Add boiling water to cover. Add salt, ginger, allspice, onion, and carrot. Bring to a boil. Cover and simmer over low heat 3 hours. Cool meat in broth 30 minutes. Remove meat from broth; place in a nonmetal, 9-inch square dish. Cover with plastic wrap or waxed paper. Place another 9-inch square dish on top of meat. Place several cans of food in top dish. Refrigerate overnight. Meat roll may be wrapped airtight and frozen. For best flavor, thaw in wrapper in refrigerator. To serve, remove string and cut in ¼-inch slices. Makes about 30 slices.

Home-Cured Christmas Ham
Julskinka—Scandinavia

This home-cured ham will not be as salty as commercially prepared hams. You can find curing salt in the baking sections of most supermarkets.

1 fresh leg of pork (12 to 14 pounds)
2 tablespoons brown sugar
8½ cups meat-curing salt (divided)
10 quarts water

Rye Crust:

About 1½ cups water
6 cups rye flour
4 to 6 small baking apples
½ pound large pitted prunes

Mustard-Crumb Coating

½ cup coarse-grain Dijon mustard
2 cups fine dry breadcrumbs
1 cup packed brown sugar
2 teaspoons ground ginger

Royal Icing and Garnish

2 teaspoons powdered egg white plus 2 tablespoons water (to make
   1 egg white)
3 cups powdered sugar
1 small red apple, polished
1 small orange, same size as apple

Remove skin and most of fat from pork. In a small bowl, combine brown sugar and ½ cup of the curing salt. Rub mixture over entire surface of ham. Place ham in a deep, nonmetal container deep enough to hold ham covered with brine (brine is added later). Cover and refrigerate 2 days. In a large pot, combine 10 quarts water with 8 cups curing salt. Bring to a boil over high heat; stir until salt is dissolved. Cool; pour brine over ham. If necessary, add more water to cover ham completely. Refrigerate 10 days. Rinse ham in cold water, using several changes of water; pat dry. Preheat oven to 300°F. In a large bowl, stir enough water into the rye flour to make a stiff dough. Turn out onto a lightly floured board; knead until smooth. Dough may be sticky. Roll out dough to an 18-inch square or large enough to encase ham. Place ham on dough; fold dough around ham, covering completely. Insert meat thermometer into thickest part of ham, not touching bone. Place ham on a rack in a shallow roasting pan. Bake 5 hours or until thermometer registers 175°F. After about 4 hours, place baking apples in a 9-inch square baking pan. Bake 1 hour or until apples are tender, but not broken. Cook prunes as directed on package; cool and drain. Remove crust from baked ham; reserve for dipping, if desired.

Smear the ham with the mustard evenly. Combine breadcrumbs, brown sugar, and ginger. Pat mixture over ham to make an even coating. Return ham to oven for 10 to 15 minutes or until crumbs are browned and crisp. Press apple onto the pointed end of a 12-inch wooden skewer. Press orange onto pointed end of the same skewer. Using 1½ yards of red ribbon, tie ribbon to blunt end of skewer and set aside.

To prepare the Royal Icing, use a small bowl to mix the powdered egg white and water with the powdered sugar until smooth. Add water if necessary to make a soft icing. Spoon icing into a pastry bag with a thin writing tip. Or, spoon icing into a 1-pint-sized heavy plastic bag with a zip-top closing. With scissors, cut across one corner to make a fine hole. Pipe icing in a crisscross pattern over the ham. Place ham on a platter. Garnish with cooked prunes and baked apples. Insert pointed end of skewer into shank end of ham. Makes 25 servings.

Baked Mushrooms

Paistettu Sienet—Finland

Mushrooms, especially wild ones, appear often in Finnish meals.

¼ cup butter
2 pounds mushrooms, quartered
1 green onion, chopped
½ teaspoon salt
¼ teaspoon freshly ground black pepper
2 tablespoons all-purpose flour
½ cup water
½ cup whipping cream
¼ cup soft breadcrumbs

Preheat oven to 450°F (230°C). Butter a shallow 2-quart baking dish; set aside. Melt butter in a large skillet. Add mushrooms and green onion; sauté 5 minutes over high heat, stirring occasionally. Sprinkle with salt, pepper, and flour; stir to blend. Pour mushroom mixture into prepared baking dish; set aside. Pour water into skillet. Bring to a boil over high heat; stir until drippings are blended to make a sauce. Pour over mushrooms. Pour whipping cream over mushrooms. Sprinkle with breadcrumbs. Bake 10 minutes or until bubbly. Makes 8 servings.

Christmas Salad

Julsallad—Scandinavia

The fresh flavors in this salad blend and season it without additional spices.

1 large green apple, cored, diced
1 cup finely chopped pickled beets
2 cups finely shredded red cabbage
1 tablespoon lemon juice
Dash salt
Lettuce

In a large bowl, combine apple, beets, cabbage, lemon juice, and salt. Cover and refrigerate until chilled. Line a serving plate or platter with lettuce; top with cabbage mixture. Makes 8 servings.

Winter Salad

Vintersallad—Swedish

This crisp, tangy salad can be prepared in advance.

  2 grapefruit
  2 heads Belgian endive
  2 cups finely shredded white cabbage
  2 green onions, thinly sliced
  ⅓ cup frozen orange juice concentrate, thawed

Section grapefruit by removing peel and all of white portion. Cut on both sides of membranes separating sections. Lift out fruit. Remove and reserve large outer leaves from endive; slice center portion into thin shreds. In a large bowl, combine grapefruit sections, sliced endive, cabbage, and green onions. Stir in orange juice concentrate. Spoon into a medium serving bowl. Tuck reserved outer leaves from endive around edge of salad. Cover and refrigerate 3 to 4 hours before serving. Makes about 8 servings.

Marinated Oranges

Marinerte Appelsiner—Norway

A mild garlic-flavored marinade brings out the subtle flavor of fresh orange slices.

  8 seedless oranges
  1 garlic clove, minced or pressed
  3 tablespoons vegetable oil
  ⅛ teaspoon white pepper
  Minced fresh rosemary for garnish

Peel oranges, removing all of white portion. Cut into ⅓-inch slices. Arrange in an overlapping pattern on a shallow platter. In a small bowl, blend garlic, oil, and white pepper. Drizzle over orange slices. Sprinkle with rosemary. Cover and refrigerate 1 hour. Makes 8 servings.

Christmas Rice Pudding

Julgrøt—Scandinavia

There are many versions of this favorite pudding.

¾ cup medium-grain rice, uncooked
½ teaspoon salt
1½ cups boiling water
2 cups whipping cream
2 cups milk
1 cinnamon stick (3 inches)
2 eggs, beaten
1 tablespoon butter
⅓ cup sugar
½ teaspoon freshly ground cardamom
1 whole almond, shelled, blanched
½ cup sugar
1 tablespoon ground cinnamon
1 to 2 cups half-and-half

Preheat oven to 325°F (165°C). Butter a deep 2-quart casserole dish; set aside. In a medium saucepan, combine rice, salt, and boiling water. Cover and simmer over low heat 10 minutes. Stir in whipping cream, milk, cinnamon stick, eggs, butter, ⅓ cup sugar, cardamom, and almond. Spoon rice mixture into prepared casserole dish. Bake 2 hours or until rice swells and has a creamy texture. In a small bowl, combine ½ cup sugar and 1 tablespoon cinnamon. Serve pudding hot or cold with half-and-half and cinnamon-sugar mixture. Makes 8 to 12 servings.

Norwegian Cream Pudding

Rømmegrøt—Norway

To make this delicious, smooth pudding, purchase the richest cream possible.

2 cups rich whipping cream	2 tablespoons sugar
⅓ cup all-purpose flour	1 tablespoon ground cinnamon
1½ cups milk	½ cup sugar
½ teaspoon salt	

Pour cream into a heavy 3- or 4-quart saucepan; bring to a boil over medium heat. Place flour in a sifter or strainer. While sifting flour into cream, beat with a whisk, keeping mixture smooth. Beat mixture with a wooden spoon as it cooks over low heat. Cook and stir 15 minutes or until mixture is thickened, comes away from the side of the pan, and is reduced in volume. Continue to cook and stir until butterfat separates from flour mixture. Pour butterfat into a small serving dish to serve later. Rich cream will produce at least ½ cup butterfat. Slowly stir in milk, salt, and 2 tablespoons sugar; heat until mixture comes to a boil. Beat with a whisk until smooth. If lumps will not smooth out, pour mixture through a strainer, or process in a blender or food processor until smooth. In a small bowl, stir cinnamon into ½ cup sugar. Serve hot pudding in dessert bowls. Serve with rendered butterfat and cinnamon-sugar mixture. Makes 6 to 8 servings.

Note: Ultra-pasteurized cream does not separate during cooking. If your cream does not separate, serve melted Clarified Butter (see below) with pudding.

Clarified Butter

Melt any amount of salted or unsalted butter in a heavy, medium saucepan over low heat. Butter will separate as it heats. Cook until milky portion at the bottom evaporates. Do not let mixture brown. Place a fine strainer or sieve lined with several layers of cheesecloth over a glass jar. Pour remaining oily mixture through strainer or sieve. Cover jar; store in refrigerator up to 4 weeks or in freezer up to 4 months.

❀Celebrations

May Day Brunch Buffet

May Day Crullers

Sliced Cooked Ham

Cheese Casserole

Cardamom Coffee Braid (page 242)

Rye-Meal Bread (page 246)

Crisp Cheese Sticks

Lemon Sparkle, Coffee

WELCOME SPRING! When spring arrives, Scandinavia bursts into color and action. Winter is gone and summer is yet to come. May Day eve, or *Walpurgis night,* is celebrated with *fire festivals.* Huge bonfires are set on the highest hill available so they can be seen at great distances. It was an old pagan belief that bonfires and noise would drive away evil spirits, wolves, and witches.

In old Sweden, *egg-singing* was a custom practiced on Walpurgis night. Young people would march from farm to farm, stopping outside each home to sing the twenty-eight verses of an old May Day song about the wonders of spring, summer, and being young. If they were well received, the singers would place a green twig on the roof of the house—a symbol of fertility. In return, the farmer paid them with fresh eggs.

Finns are normally quiet, but on the eve of May Day, there is much laughing, singing, and partying. It is the time to savor good food and to play old-fashioned games such as *drop the handkerchief,* and to dance around the maypole. Both grown-ups and children carry huge, colorful balloons purchased from sidewalk vendors. Starting on the evening of

April 30, students don white caps and dance, sing, and party until the next morning.

May Day is the time to drop in on friends and enjoy their *Sima,* a lemon-flavored beverage made bubbly with yeast. Crisp *Tippaleipä,* similar to funnel cake, is served with Sima. Traditionally, both are served only for May Day. About that time of year, both of these treats are available in coffee shops in Finland. They are not hard to make. Start the Sima several days in advance to give the flavor time to develop. Tippaleipä is a deep-fried pastry that is best eaten just after frying. Guests can even fry their own. This is a perfect back porch or patio activity.

The substantial part of your buffet includes ham or another cooked meat and *Ost Låda,* a Swedish cheese casserole. Assemble the casserole and refrigerate it overnight. Let it sit at room temperature for 30 minutes before baking.

May Day Crullers
Tippaleipä—Finland

These "bird's nests" are similar to funnel cakes.

1 envelope active dry yeast (¼ ounce)
2 tablespoons warm water (110°F, 45°C)
2 eggs
1 tablespoon granulated sugar
1 cup milk, scalded, cooled
½ teaspoon salt
2 cups all-purpose flour
Oil for deep-frying
Powdered sugar, sifted

In a small bowl, stir yeast into water; let stand 3 to 4 minutes to soften. In a large bowl, beat eggs and granulated sugar until blended. Stir in milk, yeast mixture, and salt. Using a whisk, beat in flour until mixture is smooth. Cover bowl with a dry towel; set in a warm place to rise until bubbly, 45 to 60 minutes. In a large skillet, pour oil for deep-frying 1½ to 2 inches deep. Over medium-high heat, bring oil to 375°F (190°C). Pour 1 cup batter into a pastry bag fitted with a ¼-inch tip, a heavy plastic bag with a ¼-inch opening cut in a corner, or a squeezable plastic bottle with a narrow tip. Squeeze batter through opening into hot oil, swirling in a circular design similar to a *bird's nest,* 3 to 4 inches in diameter. Fry 1 minute on each side or until golden brown. Use a slotted spoon to lift cooked crullers from hot oil. Drain on paper towels. Dust with powdered sugar. Serve hot. Makes 15 crullers.

Cheese Casserole

Ost Låda—Sweden

Very much like a crustless quiche.

    8 Swedish anchovy fillets
    2 cups shredded Gouda or Jarlsberg cheese (8 ounces)
    4 eggs
    2 cups half-and-half
    2 tablespoons chopped fresh parsley

Butter a 9- or 10-inch quiche pan or shallow casserole dish. Preheat oven to 350°F (175°C). Arrange anchovies over bottom of prepared pan or dish. Sprinkle cheese over top. In a medium bowl, beat eggs; stir in half-and-half. Pour egg mixture over cheese and anchovies. Bake 25 minutes or until golden brown around edge. Sprinkle with parsley. Serve hot or cool. Makes 6 servings.

Crisp Cheese Sticks

Oststänger—Sweden

Serve these crispy sticks with salads or soups.

¼ cup butter, room temperature
½ cup all-purpose flour
½ cup shredded Swiss, Cheddar, or Edam cheese (2 ounces)
1 to 2 tablespoons water, if necessary
1 egg, beaten
¼ cup poppy, caraway, or sesame seeds

Generously grease a jelly-roll pan; set aside. Preheat oven to 375°F (190°C). In a small bowl, combine butter, flour, and cheese until mixture forms a ball; if needed, stir in 1 to 2 tablespoons water. Refrigerate 20 minutes. On a lightly floured board, roll out dough to a 12 x 10-inch rectangle. Cut in 4 x 2-inch strips. Twist strips 2 to 4 times. Dip in beaten egg, then in seeds. Arrange on prepared pan. Bake 8 to 10 minutes until crisp and golden brown. Makes 15 cheese sticks.

Lemon Sparkle

Sima—Finland

Beer adds an authentic malt-like flavor to this refreshing, sparkling drink.

2 lemons
4 quarts water
3 cups packed brown sugar
1 teaspoon active dry yeast
¼ teaspoon ground ginger
1 bottle light beer (12 ounces), if desired
8 teaspoons granulated sugar
1 tablespoon raisins

Wash and dry lemons. Use a vegetable peeler to cut yellow zest from peel; set aside. Remove and discard all white pith from lemons. Cut peeled lemons in thin slices. In a 5- to 6-quart saucepan, bring water to a boil over high heat. Stir in brown sugar until dissolved. Add lemon peel and sliced lemons. Remove from heat; cool. Pour into a large nonmetal container. Stir in yeast, ginger, and beer, if desired. Cover and let stand at room temperature overnight or until tiny bubbles form around edge. Sterilize pint or quart bottles or a gallon bottle. Scald caps, lids, or corks in boiling water. Spoon granulated sugar and a few raisins into each bottle or jar, adding 1 teaspoon sugar for each pint of liquid. Strain liquid before pouring into sterile bottles. Attach sterile caps, lids, or corks. Let stand at room temperature until raisins rise to top, 8 hours to 2 days. Refrigerate until ready to serve. Serve cold. Makes about 4 quarts.

Norwegian Independence Day Buffet

MENU

Cheese Mousse, Crisp Crackers

Potato Flatbread (page 45)

Fish Mousse with Shrimp Sauce

Jarlsberg Cod

Smörgås Salad Platter

Trondheim Lemon-Raisin Soup

Cardamom Crackers

Fruit-Juice Glögg (page 159)

Mineral Water, Beer

ON THE SEVENTEENTH OF MAY, up go the Norwegian flags. Choirs sing. Bands march in parades. Not only is *Syttende Mai* the anniversary of the Norwegian Constitution—adopted at Eidsvall in 1814—but it is the awakening of new life after long winter months.

The celebration is particularly merry in northern Norway, where winters are long and cold. A famous celebration is held in the little village of Rjukan, situated in a narrow valley between mountains six thousand feet high. Rjukan has no sun from late fall to the middle of March. The highlight of the festival is the arrival of the *Prince of the Sun,* who ascends his throne and issues the order of the day: "Let there be merriment until dawn!"

And merriment there is, as young and old dance in carnival costumes. Fireworks and bonfires are traditional, and hearken back to pagan customs of chasing away evil spirits.

Lefse is one of the typical foods served for Syttende Mai. Lefse is served at all special occasions in Norway. It belongs on a celebration menu whether it is for Syttende Mai, a wedding, or an anniversary. Lefse is especially good with Fish Mousse. Nobody makes Fish Mousse like a Norwegian! Light in texture and wonderfully flavored, the creation is beautiful to look at when oven-poached in a pretty ring mold.

As you plan a dinner party around this menu, choose between Fish Mousse with Shrimp Sauce and Jarlsberg Cod. The other offerings will complement either of these main dishes.

Cheese Mousse

Oste Fromage—Norway

Serve this as an appetizer spread for crackers and flatbreads.

1 envelope unflavored gelatin (¼ ounce)
½ cup cold water
⅔ cup half-and-half
3 egg yolks, slightly beaten
4 ounces Danish blue cheese, crumbled
¾ cup whipping cream, whipped
Radishes, watercress, and black olives for garnish

Lightly oil a 2- to 2½-cup decorative mold; set aside. In a small bowl, sprinkle gelatin over cold water; set aside to soften. In a heavy, medium saucepan, combine half-and-half and egg yolks. Stir with a whisk over low heat until mixture cooks and thickens. Stir in softened gelatin and blue cheese; whisk until mixture is smooth. Refrigerate until texture resembles unbeaten egg whites, 30 to 45 minutes. Fold in whipped cream. Pour into prepared mold. Cover and refrigerate until set, 3 to 4 hours. Invert onto a round, medium platter; garnish with radishes, watercress, and olives. Makes about 2 cups or 12 servings.

To determine the volume of a baking dish or mold, pour in water, 1 cup at a time, to within ¼ inch of the rim.

Fish Mousse

Fiskepudding—Norway

This is the highlight of Norwegian cuisine—wonderfully light, airy, and beautiful.

1½ pounds fresh or frozen pike, sole, haddock, or cod fillets
2 teaspoons salt
¼ teaspoon ground white pepper
Dash ground nutmeg
1½ tablespoons cornstarch
1⅓ cups milk
1½ cups whipping cream
1 tablespoon butter
About ¼ cup soft breadcrumbs
Chopped fresh parsley
Shrimp Sauce (page 106)

Thaw frozen fish. Skin and bone fish, if necessary. Use paper towels to wipe fish dry. Cut fish crosswise into strips. Put fish strips through food grinder 3 times or until pureed. In large bowl of electric mixer, combine pureed fish, salt, pepper, nutmeg, and cornstarch. Beat with electric mixer on high speed 10 minutes. Beat 20 minutes longer, gradually beating in milk and whipping cream. Or, use a food processor fitted with a steel blade: turn processor on, then drop fish fillets through feed tube. Process until pureed, adding salt, pepper, nutmeg, and cornstarch, and then gradually pour in milk and cream. If processor bowl is small, process in batches. Continue processing until mixture is light and fluffy. Preheat oven to 375°F (190°C). Butter a 10-cup ring mold or fancy tube mold and coat with breadcrumbs. Butter center of a 12-inch square of parchment paper, waxed paper, or foil. Gently spoon whipped fish mixture into mold. Cover with buttered paper or foil, lightly pressing onto surface of fish mixture. Place mold in a 13 x 9-inch baking dish. Pour boiling water 1 inch deep into baking dish. Bake 45 minutes or until mixture pulls away from side of pan and a knife inserted in center comes out clean. Prepare Shrimp Sauce while mold bakes. Invert hot mousse onto a warmed serving dish. Sprinkle with chopped parsley. Serve immediately with hot Shrimp Sauce. Makes 8 servings.

Shrimp Sauce

Rekesaus—Norway

This is excellent served with poached fish or Norwegian Fish Mousse (page 104).

¼ cup butter
¼ cup all-purpose flour
¼ cup whipping cream
2 cups milk
1½ teaspoons salt
¼ teaspoon white pepper
2 tablespoons sherry, if desired
2 pounds cooked, tiny shrimp
2 tablespoons dried dill weed or chopped fresh dill

Melt butter in a medium saucepan; stir in flour. Add cream and milk, whisking to keep mixture smooth. Cook and stir over medium heat until thickened and smooth. Stir in salt, pepper, and sherry, if desired. Add shrimp, stirring occasionally, and cook until shrimp are heated through. Stir in dill. Serve hot. Makes 4 cups.

Jarlsberg Cod

Jarlsberg Torsk—Norway

Creamy Jarlsberg cheese and tomatoes make a delicious topping for baked cod.

1½ pounds fresh or frozen cod fillets
1 tablespoon butter
2 teaspoons salt
1 teaspoon ground white pepper
4 tomatoes, sliced
2 cups shredded Jarlsberg or baby Swiss cheese (8 ounces)
½ cup whipping cream

Thaw frozen fish. Remove skin and bones, if necessary. Use paper towels to wipe fish dry. Preheat oven to 375°F (190°C). Spread butter over bottom of a 13 x 9-inch baking dish. Arrange dry fish in dish. Sprinkle with salt and white pepper. Top with tomato slices, covering fish completely. Sprinkle with cheese and pour cream over top. Bake 25 minutes or until fish flakes when pierced with a fork. Makes 4 servings.

Smörgås Salad Platter

Salatsauser med Rømme—Norway

Guests make their own salads from this lovely presentation of fresh vegetables.

    Cream Dressing (see below)
    2 heads Boston, butter, or Bibb lettuce
    1 large avocado, sliced and sprinkled with lemon juice
    2 tomatoes, cut in thin wedges
    2 cups sliced mushrooms
    1 can pickled beets (16 ounces), cut in julienne strips
    1 cup sliced radishes
    ½ cup sliced green onions
    ½ pound spinach, washed and shredded

Cream Dressing
    1 cup whipping cream
    2 tablespoons chili sauce
    ½ teaspoon salt
    ¼ teaspoon ground white pepper
    Curry powder to taste

Prepare Cream Dressing; refrigerate until chilled. Arrange vegetables on a salad platter. Cover and refrigerate until ready to serve. To serve, have guests assemble their own salads, selecting from offerings on platter and topping with Cream Dressing. Makes 10 to 12 servings.

Cream Dressing
In a small bowl, beat cream until stiff peaks form. Fold in remaining ingredients.

Trondheim Lemon-Raisin Soup

Trondhjem Suppe—Norway

This slightly sweet, faintly lemon soup makes a perfect luncheon, supper, or dessert dish.

6 cups boiling water
½ cup short- or medium-grain rice, uncooked
1 cup light or dark raisins
3 tablespoons fresh lemon juice
2 tablespoons sugar
½ cup whipping cream
⅛ teaspoon salt
2 egg yolks, beaten

In a 3- or 4-quart saucepan, combine water, rice, and raisins. Bring to a boil over high heat. Reduce heat to low; simmer 20 minutes or until rice is tender. In a small bowl, combine lemon juice, sugar, cream, salt, and egg yolks. Add lemon mixture to hot soup, slowly beating with a whisk. Serve hot or cold. Makes 8 servings.

Cardamom Crackers

Goro—Norway

Make these on a "goro" iron (page xv), then break the crackers into three pieces.

    3 eggs
    1 cup sugar
    1 cup whipping cream, whipped
    1 cup butter, melted
    ¼ teaspoon salt
    1 teaspoon ground cardamom
    6 cups all-purpose flour

Cut a paper pattern the same size as the goro iron; set aside. In a large bowl, combine all ingredients in the order given, mixing until thoroughly blended. Dough will be stiff. Divide dough into 4 equal pieces. On a lightly floured surface, roll out each piece to a rectangle ⅛ to ¹⁄₁₆ inch thick. Cut the same size and shape as the paper pattern. Place goro iron on stovetop over medium heat until a drop of water sizzles and bounces when dropped on iron. Brush inside of iron with shortening. Place 1 piece of cut-out dough on hot iron. Close iron and bake over medium heat 1 to 2 minutes on each side until golden brown. Remove crackers from iron. Cool on a rack; repeat with remaining dough. Separate into individual crackers. Makes about 36 crackers.

Nameday Dinner

MENU

Herring Cocktail

Swedish Limpa (page 248)

Swedish Mushroom Soup

Crisp Cheese Sticks (page 99)

Royal Pot Roast of Beef

Hasselback Potatoes

Steamed Vegetable Platter

Mocha Torte

Red or White Wine, Coffee, Tea

IN SWEDEN AND FINLAND, it is traditional to celebrate your *nameday* rather than your *birthday*. This is a legacy of times past. Birthday celebrations were discouraged. But people were allowed to celebrate the day of the saint after which they were named. For instance, if your name was Beatrice, you would observe St. Beatrice's Day on the second day of December.

Today, namedays are convenient when people do not want to give their ages. Children observe birthdays up to their teens, but most Scandinavian women celebrate their nameday. Men celebrate their nameday until they reach fifty.

When a man has his fiftieth birthday, a great celebration is planned. The more prominent the person is in the community or country, the bigger the party. He invites all his friends, work associates, and relatives to celebrate his marking of a half-century. Some men have a big reception at a hotel or public place. Many have an open house at home with a several-course meal. There is toasting with champagne and gifts. Because of the expense, some families plan and save for years for this special occasion.

The suggested menu is not lavish, but it is festive. You may serve all the courses, or choose only one dish and a dessert from this party-for-eight menu. To serve it Scandinavian style, there must be toasting with champagne, or with the traditional schnapps and beer.

Schnapps should be gulped in one swallow, followed by beer as a chaser. Schnapps glasses hold about two tablespoons of liquid. After gulping, you are to hold the glass upside down on top of your head to show that it is empty. When I expressed hesitancy to gulp it, I was politely told it is all right for ladies to sip. What a relief!

Herring Cocktail

Sillcocktail—Sweden

Serve this first course in stemmed glasses, punch cups, or small dessert bowls.

1 jar herring tidbits in wine sauce (8 ounces)
4 medium potatoes, peeled and boiled
8 butter or Boston lettuce leaves
½ cup dairy sour cream
¼ teaspoon salt
⅛ teaspoon ground white pepper
1 tablespoon minced green onion
1 teaspoon lemon juice
Dried dill weed, fresh dill sprigs, or chopped chives

Drain herring. Slice potatoes about ¼ inch thick. Place a lettuce leaf in each of 8 small dishes. Dividing evenly, arrange sliced potatoes and drained herring on lettuce. In a small bowl, combine sour cream, salt, pepper, green onion, and lemon juice. Spoon a dollop of sour cream mixture on top of each serving. Garnish with dill or chives. Makes 8 servings.

Swedish Mushroom Soup

Svampsoppa—Sweden

If chanterelle mushrooms are available in your area, they are excellent in this soup.

3 tablespoons butter
1 pound fresh mushrooms, thinly sliced
½ teaspoon salt
¼ teaspoon ground white pepper
⅓ cup all-purpose flour
About 8 cups (64 ounces) beef or chicken broth
1 cup whipping cream
1 teaspoon lemon juice
Salt and ground white pepper to taste
¼ cup dry sherry

Melt butter in a 3- to 4-quart heavy saucepan over low heat. Add mushrooms; sauté over low heat until mushroom juices begin to flow. Pour mushroom juice into a 2-cup measuring cup; set aside. Stir salt, white pepper, and flour into drained mushrooms. Add enough broth to mushroom juice to make 2 cups. Stir into mushroom mixture. Stir in 6 cups of remaining broth. Over high heat, cook and stir until soup is thickened, about 5 minutes. Stir in cream and lemon juice. Add salt and white pepper to taste. Stir in sherry. Serve hot. Makes 8 servings.

Royal Pot Roast of Beef

Slottsstek—Sweden

Flaming brandy adds flavor to the roast and to the drippings.

1 teaspoon salt
1 teaspoon ground allspice
½ teaspoon freshly ground black pepper
1 boneless beef chuck roast (4 to 4½ pounds)
3 tablespoons butter
3 tablespoons brandy, if desired
⅓ cup beef broth
2 medium onions, sliced
3 anchovy fillets, minced
2 bay leaves
2 tablespoons white wine vinegar
2 tablespoons dark corn syrup

Combine salt, allspice, and pepper. Rub over entire surface of beef. Melt butter in a 6-quart Dutch oven or heavy stewing pot. Add meat; brown on all sides. If used, pour brandy into a small saucepan. Warm over low heat; ignite. Pour over meat. Add broth, onions, anchovies, bay leaves, vinegar, and corn syrup. Cover pot. Simmer over very low heat for 2 hours or until tender. Place beef on a platter; keep warm. Pour drippings through a strainer into a large bowl. Return strained drippings to pot. Stir occasionally over medium-high heat, boiling until only 2 cups of drippings remain. Spoon about ¼ cup drippings over beef as a glaze. Pour remaining drippings into a serving bowl and serve with roast. Makes 8 servings.

Hasselback Potatoes

Hasselbackpotatis—Sweden

These attractive scored potatoes can be baked in a roasting pan with any roast. They were first served at the Hasselback restaurant in Stockholm.

6 to 8 baking potatoes
¼ cup butter, melted
About 1 teaspoon salt
¼ cup fine dry breadcrumbs

Butter a 13 x 9-inch baking dish; set aside. Preheat oven to 400°F (205°C). Peel potatoes; place in ice water to prevent browning. Dry 1 potato at a time with paper towels. Place dry potato in a ladle or deep spoon. Using a sharp knife, slice potato crosswise in ⅛-inch slices only to edge of ladle or spoon, not all the way through. Return scored potatoes to ice water. Drain on paper towels. Arrange potatoes, cut-side up, in prepared dish. Brush with half of butter; sprinkle with salt. Bake 30 minutes or until tender. Brush with remaining butter; sprinkle with crumbs. Bake 15 minutes longer or until browned. Makes 6 to 8 servings.

Steamed Vegetable Platter

Grønsaksfat—Scandinavian

The variety of vegetables makes a pretty platter.

> 1 cauliflower head (1½ to 2 pounds), trimmed
> Boiling water
> 1½ pounds broccoli, tough ends trimmed
> ½ to 1 pound zucchini squash, cut into ¼-inch slices
> 1 pound carrots, peeled, cooked, and diagonally cut into ¼-inch slices
> ¼ cup butter, melted
> 1 teaspoon dried leaf tarragon or basil
> Salt and pepper to taste

Place whole cauliflower in a deep, large saucepan; add 1 inch boiling water. Cover; cook over medium heat 5 minutes. Add broccoli; cook 5 minutes. Add zucchini; cook 5 minutes. Drain vegetables; arrange cooked cauliflower, broccoli, zucchini, and carrots on a large platter. Drizzle with butter; sprinkle with tarragon or basil and salt and pepper to taste. Makes 8 servings.

Use the cooking water from fresh vegetables as the liquid for baking yeast breads or add it to homemade soup for flavor and nutrition.

Mocha Torte

Mockatårta—Sweden

This lovely meringue layer cake has a smooth, mild, coffee-flavored filling.

Meringue Layers (see below)
⅓ cup ground coffee beans
½ cup water
1 cup half-and-half
3 egg yolks, slightly beaten
1½ tablespoons cornstarch
1 cup unsalted butter, room temperature
1 cup powdered sugar
1 teaspoon vanilla extract
⅓ cup slivered almonds, toasted

Meringue Layers

4 egg whites
½ teaspoon cream of tartar
1¼ cups sugar

Prepare Meringue Layers. In a small saucepan, bring coffee and water to a boil; remove from heat and let steep 5 minutes. Place a strainer over the top of a double boiler. Line strainer with a coffee filter. Pour coffee mixture into strainer. Discard coffee grounds. To coffee liquid, add half-and-half, egg yolks, and cornstarch. Beating with an electric mixer on high speed, cook over simmering water until mixture is thick and smooth. Cover pan; set aside. In the small bowl of an electric mixer, cream butter and sugar; add vanilla. Beat in coffee mixture, 1 tablespoon at a time, until smooth and fluffy. If mixture begins to curdle, place bowl over hot water and continue beating until smooth and fluffy. Cool to room temperature. Place a meringue layer on a round platter. Spread 1 cup filling over top. Place second meringue on top. Spread remaining filling over top. Sprinkle with almonds. Refrigerate at least 3 hours before serving. Makes 16 small servings.

Meringue Layers

Grease and flour a large baking sheet. Draw 2 circles (9 inches) in flour on baking sheet. Preheat oven to 250°F (120°C). In a large bowl, beat egg whites until frothy. Add cream of tartar. Beat constantly while adding sugar, 1 tablespoon at a time. Beat until stiff and dry. Spread half of meringue in each circle on baking sheet, making flat and even. Bake 2 to 2½ hours or until meringues are a creamy yellow color. Turn off oven. Leave meringues in closed oven to cool.

❀Dinners and Buffets

Danish Roast Beef Buffet

MENU

Savory Tartlets

Danablu Tomatoes

Danish Roast Beef

or

Spiced Danish Meatballs

Danish Red Cabbage

Caramelized Carrots or Potatoes

Mocha Mousse

Aquavit, Schnapps, Danish Beer, Milk, Coffee

IT IS WITH GREAT AND CALCULATED CARE that tiny Denmark produces food. The average Danish farm is only 25 acres, but is an excellent example of efficiency. Three-fourths of the total acreage of Denmark is devoted to agriculture. Of that, ten percent is used for hay, oats, rye, wheat, and root crops. Almost all of the Danish farm income comes from animal products—butter, cheese, pork, beef, poultry, and eggs. Denmark produces more beef than any other Scandinavian country.

As you drive through the Danish countryside, you see little *gaards*, or farms, nestled in the slightly rolling hills. A U-shaped cluster of thatch-roofed, whitewashed buildings forms the hub of the gaard. It is so neat and tidy it is difficult to pick out the house from the barn. The buildings include the farmhouse, cow barn, pig stall, and machine shed. The center of the U is a neat little courtyard.

Charming Danish *kroers* or country inns, sidewalk cafes, and restaurants offer an elaborate and creative variety of cuisines. Danes love good food. Homecooked meals are plain and thrifty. They are always tasty and beautifully presented, even to family members around the cloth-covered kitchen table.

When guests are invited, the meal is planned as lavishly as for a king. The host takes great pains to set a beautiful table. With imagination and an artistic eye, he or she skillfully arranges flowers, candles, and flags. Lovely porcelain figurines may set off classic blue and white Royal Copenhagen china. The meal becomes an evening of entertainment around the table. Talk and laughter begin and end the meal, with jokes and stories interspersed.

Danish cuisine reflects a more continental flare than the rest of Scandinavia. It is characterized by careful attention to seasoning and detail, and a feel for adventure.

For a festive occasion, serve schnapps as the Danes do, in tiny cordial glasses. Provide good Danish beer as a chaser. They also serve red wine, mineral water, milk, buttermilk, and juices.

Savory Tartlets

Tarteletter—Denmark

For a pretty presentation, make all three fillings.

    1½ cups all-purpose flour
    ½ cup butter
    ¼ teaspoon salt
    1 egg, beaten
    2 teaspoons lemon juice
    1 to 2 tablespoons ice water
    Choice of fillings (see below)

Ham and Spinach Filling

    2 tablespoons butter
    2 tablespoons all-purpose flour
    1 cup half-and-half or milk
    1 cup finely diced cooked ham
    1 package frozen chopped spinach (10 ounces), cooked, squeezed dry

Crab and Shrimp Filling

    2 tablespoons butter
    1 tablespoon all-purpose flour
    1 package frozen snow crab (8 ounces), thawed
    1 teaspoon anchovy paste
    ¼ pound or 1 package frozen tiny cocktail shrimp (4 ounces), thawed,
        drained
    Paprika

Mushroom Filling

    2 tablespoons butter
    ¼ pound mushrooms, sliced
    1 tablespoon all-purpose flour
    ½ teaspoon salt

¼ teaspoon ground allspice
1 tablespoon dry sherry
Chopped fresh parsley

In a medium bowl or food processor fitted with a steel blade, blend flour, butter, and salt until mixture resembles coarse crumbs. In a small bowl, combine egg, lemon juice, and 1 tablespoon ice water. Stir into flour mixture only until moistened. Add more ice water, if necessary. Gather dough into a ball. Wrap in plastic wrap; refrigerate 30 minutes. Divide dough into fourths. On a lightly floured board, roll out one-fourth of dough until it is ⅛ inch thick. Arrange 6 *sandbakelser* or *tartlet tins* (1½ inches wide) close together near board. Wrap rolled-out dough around rolling pin. Without stretching dough, lift and gently unroll over tins. Gently lift and drape dough so it falls into tins. Roll rolling pin firmly over tins, cutting dough. Remove excess dough. Press dough evenly into each tin, from bottom to top, so dough reaches top of mold. Do not let dough extend above top of mold. Pierce bottoms of shells with a fork. Repeat with remaining dough. Refrigerate 30 minutes. Prepare filling or fillings; set aside. Preheat oven to 400°F (205°C). Bake chilled pastry shells 8 to 10 minutes until golden. Cool 10 minutes in tins, then remove from tins. Spoon fillings into shells. Makes 24 tartlets.

Ham and Spinach Filling
Melt butter in a small saucepan over medium heat. Stir in flour until blended. Gradually stir in half-and-half or milk. Stir until sauce is thickened. Stir in ham and spinach. Makes 3 cups.

Crab and Shrimp Filling
Melt butter in a small saucepan over medium heat. Stir in flour; add crabmeat and liquid. Stir until thickened. Stir in anchovy paste and shrimp. Sprinkle with paprika. Makes 2½ cups.

Mushroom Filling
Melt butter in a medium skillet over high heat. Add mushrooms; sauté until browned, 4 to 5 minutes. Sprinkle flour, salt, and allspice over sautéed mushrooms; cook and stir until juices are thickened. Stir in sherry. Sprinkle with chopped parsley. Makes about 2½ cups.

Danablu Tomatoes

Tomater med Danablu—Denmark

Tomatoes stuffed with a combination of apples, celery, and blue cheese—very tasty!

8 firm, medium tomatoes
1 large Golden Delicious or Winesap apple, unpeeled, chopped
8 pimiento-stuffed green olives, chopped
1 celery stalk, minced
4 ounces Danish blue cheese, crumbled
½ cup mayonnaise
Chopped fresh parsley

Place a strainer over a small bowl; set aside. Cut a ¼-inch slice off top of each tomato to make lids. Scoop center flesh and seeds from tomatoes into strainer. Press through strainer; set aside. Discard seeds. Invert tomato shells and lids onto paper towels; let drain 10 minutes. In a medium bowl, combine apple, olives, celery, and blue cheese. Spoon evenly into drained tomatoes. Stir 2 tablespoons strained tomato into mayonnaise. Top each filled tomato with a dollop of mayonnaise mixture. Serve remaining mayonnaise mixture in a small bowl. Top each serving with reserved lids, placed slightly to one side. Garnish with chopped parsley. Makes 8 servings.

Danish Roast Beef

Oksesteg—Denmark

Select a tender cut of beef for the best results, then roast in foil to keep it juicy.

1 boneless beef loin roast (3½ to 4 pounds)
¼ cup butter, room temperature
4 garlic cloves, crushed
1 tablespoon coarsely cracked black peppercorns
1 teaspoon coarse or kosher salt

Preheat oven to 375°F (190°C). Cut a piece of heavy-duty foil large enough to wrap roast. Spread butter over center of foil. Rub roast with garlic; press pepper and salt onto surface of roast. Place meat on center of buttered foil. Bring ends of foil together, folding up against roast. Fold sides of foil to make an airtight package. Place on a rack in a roasting pan. Roast 45 minutes for rare or 1 hour for medium rare. Remove foil. Pour meat drippings into a small saucepan. Place roast on rack in roasting pan. Adjust oven temperature to 400°F (205°C). Roast 10 to 15 minutes or until meat is browned. While meat browns, place saucepan over medium-high heat. Boil drippings until reduced to a shiny glaze. Pour glaze over roast before serving. Let roast stand 20 minutes for easier slicing. Makes 8 servings.

Spiced Danish Meatballs

Krydrede Frikadeller—Denmark

Slightly flattened two-inch balls make the frikadeller authentic.

1 cup fine dry breadcrumbs
1 cup milk
2 small onions, minced
2 eggs
1½ teaspoons salt
½ teaspoon ground nutmeg
½ teaspoon ground allspice
¼ teaspoon ground cloves
¼ cup all-purpose flour
2 pounds extra-lean ground beef
2 tablespoons butter
2 tablespoons cornstarch
2 cups beef broth

In large bowl of electric mixer, blend breadcrumbs and milk. Let stand 10 minutes. Add onions, eggs, salt, nutmeg, allspice, cloves, flour, and meat. Beat with electric mixer on high speed until mixture is light and fluffy, about 10 minutes. Using ⅓ cup mixture at a time, shape like eggs. Flatten balls slightly. Melt butter in a large, heavy skillet over medium heat. Add meatballs; brown on both sides. Place cooked meatballs on a warm platter. When all are browned, add cornstarch to skillet; stir until lightly browned. Slowly stir in broth. Stir with a whisk until gravy is thickened. Place meatballs in gravy; heat through. Makes 8 servings.

When shaping meatballs or cookie dough, use a small ice-cream scoop for even portions.

Danish Red Cabbage
Rødkål—Denmark

Red cabbage is a favorite Danish side dish usually served with Christmas roast goose.

> 1 medium head red cabbage (about 1½ pounds)
> 2 tablespoons butter
> ½ cup cider vinegar, lemon juice, or pickled-beet juice
> 1 teaspoon salt
> ¼ cup sugar
> ¼ cup red currant jelly, if desired

Remove outer leaves and core from cabbage. Shred cabbage very fine. Melt butter in a large pot. Add cabbage, vinegar or juice, salt, and sugar; stir to distribute. Cover and cook over low heat until cabbage is tender, about 20 minutes. Stir in jelly, if desired. Serve hot. Makes 8 servings.

Caramelized Carrots or Potatoes
Glaserede Gulerødder i Kartoffler—Denmark

These are a wonderful accompaniment to pork or beef.

> 1½ pounds carrots, 3 to 4 inches long, or 1½ pounds small red or
>   fingerling potatoes
> ½ teaspoon salt
> Water
> ¼ cup sugar
> ¼ cup butter

Peel or scrape carrots; remove tips and stems. Peel potatoes. Place scraped carrots or peeled potatoes in a large saucepan. Add salt and water to cover. Bring to a boil over high heat. Reduce heat until water simmers. Simmer 20 minutes or until tender; drain and set aside. Heat sugar in a large heavy skillet, stirring constantly, until caramelized or lightly browned. Add butter; stir until melted. Add cooked carrots or potatoes. Shake pan or stir until evenly glazed and heated through, about 10 minutes. Serve immediately. Makes 8 servings.

Mocha Mousse

Mokkafromage—Denmark

Wonderfully rich, but light.

> 1 envelope unflavored gelatin (¼ ounce)
> ¼ cup water
> 4 ounces semisweet chocolate
> 1 teaspoon instant coffee powder
> ¼ cup powdered egg white plus ½ cup water
> ¼ cup sugar
> 1 cup whipping cream
> Whipped cream, slightly sweetened

In a small metal bowl, soften gelatin in water. Place over a pan of hot water and stir until gelatin dissolves. Add chocolate and coffee powder. Continue stirring over hot water until chocolate melts. In a large bowl, beat egg white powder and water until light and fluffy. Beat in sugar until fluffy. Fold in the chocolate mixture. Whip 1 cup whipping cream until stiff; fold into chocolate mixture. Pour into a serving dish or individual serving dishes. Serve immediately or refrigerate until chilled. Decorate with a dollop of slightly sweetened whipped cream. Makes 8 servings.

January Fish Platter

JANUARY BEGINS WITH A HOLIDAY, resolutions, cold weather, and poached cod dinners. Cod is probably the most popular and most frequently eaten of the ocean fishes. It is fished in Scandinavia in all months that have an "r" in them. Danes and Norwegians say that cod is at its best in January. The flavor is mild and the texture is perfect when poached until the flesh lies in broad, chalk-white flakes. It is also at its lowest price in January. Cod is a part of the traditional Danish New Year's Eve meal. Danes serve it with melted butter and lemon, then wash it down with beer and iced schnapps.

Norway claims to have more than two hundred varieties of fish and one way to cook them all—poaching. But fish must be absolutely fresh to satisfy Norwegian cooks. Most people buy their fish from a fishmonger, who keeps the fish alive in large water tanks. Danes use the expression, "fresh as a fish" just as other people might say "fresh as a daisy."

When we visited the quaint cobblestone-street village of Stavanger, Norway, we selected a little restaurant with an unpretentious warehouse-like front by the fishmarket and pier. After much deliberation, we chose from among the dozens of fish on the menu. While the chef tended to the poaching liquid and the rest of the menu, his assistant ran out to the market to buy the fish we had chosen. It came from the kitchen steaming hot, wonderfully fresh, and delicately flavored. We were also served a melted butter sauce and a hot mustard sauce. It was pure perfection!

For a pretty and simple presentation of this dinner, surround the cod with boiled potatoes and cooked vegetables. The only additional accompaniment you'll need is bread and butter. Dessert is a delicate Danish version of crepes stuffed with a mild orange butter. To be fancy, you can flame them with orange-flavored liqueur, or simply sprinkle the crepes with powdered sugar and reheat them under the broiler.

Poached Cod Platter

Nytårstorsk—Denmark

Serve this mild-flavored dish with Melted Butter Sauce (page 137) or Hot Mustard Sauce (page 138).

3 pounds fresh or frozen cod fillets
2 teaspoons salt
¼ cup white wine vinegar
8 cups water
¼ cup butter, melted
1 lemon, cut in wedges
18 small red or fingerling potatoes, peeled, cooked
12 small carrots, peeled, cooked
1 pound broccoli, tough ends trimmed, cooked
¼ cup chopped parsley

Thaw frozen fish. Place cod in ice water 2 hours before cooking, or 2 hours and 45 minutes before serving. Drain; sprinkle with salt. Let stand 15 minutes; rinse off salt. In a large shallow saucepan, combine vinegar and water. Bring to a boil over medium-high heat. Add fish; heat until liquid simmers. Cover pan; set aside. Let stand 20 minutes or until fish is firm but flakes when probed with a fork; drain. Arrange poached fillets on a hot platter. Pour melted butter over fish. Arrange lemon wedges, hot cooked potatoes, carrots, and broccoli around fish; sprinkle parsley over vegetables. Makes 6 servings.

If your midwinter carrots are pale, add about 1 tablespoon sugar to the cooking water to bring out a brighter color.

Dilled Shellfish

Keitetyt Ravut—Finland

This dish is always served cold with hot melted butter and lemon juice.

> 1 quart tightly packed fresh dill heads and stems
> 12 cups water
> 1 tablespoon salt
> 1 tablespoon sugar
> 3 pounds live crayfish, frozen rock or slipper lobster, or shrimp in shells
> Hot melted butter
> Lemon wedges

In a large pot, combine dill, water, salt, and sugar. Bring to a boil over medium heat; simmer 10 minutes. Add crayfish, lobster, or shrimp. Bring to a boil again. Remove from heat; let stand 15 minutes. Pour off excess liquid, leaving only enough to cover seafood. Refrigerate until chilled, 45 to 60 minutes. Drain off liquid. Arrange chilled seafood on a platter. Serve with melted butter and lemon wedges. Squeeze lemon juice over seafood; dip seafood into butter. Makes 6 servings.

Melted Butter Sauce

Smørsauce—Denmark

This sauce is excellent with any poached or baked fish.

½ cup butter
¼ cup all-purpose flour
½ teaspoon paprika
½ teaspoon salt
2 cups cold water

Melt ¼ cup butter in a medium saucepan over medium heat. Stir in flour to make a smooth paste. Stir in paprika and salt. Stir in water. Continue stirring until mixture comes to a boil; keep hot. Before serving, stir in remaining ¼ cup butter; beat until butter melts. Makes 2½ cups.

Hot Mustard Sauce

Sennepssauce—Denmark

Prepare this sauce at least 2 hours before serving to let the flavors blend.

> 3 tablespoons white wine vinegar
> 2 tablespoons coarse-grained prepared German or Swedish mustard
> 1 tablespoon dry mustard
> ¾ teaspoon salt
> ¼ teaspoon ground white pepper
> ¼ cup sugar
> ⅛ teaspoon ground cardamom
> ½ cup olive oil or vegetable oil

In a small bowl, use a whisk to beat vinegar, prepared and dry mustards, salt, white pepper, sugar, and cardamom. Gradually whisk in oil until sauce is thick. Makes about 1 cup.

Crepes with Orange Butter

Pandekager med Orangesmør—Denmark

Tender crepes accented with orange flavor complete this dinner.

1 cup all-purpose flour
Pinch salt
2 eggs, slightly beaten
1 cup milk
⅓ cup butter, melted
Shortening
Citrus-Flavored Butter (see below)
½ cup orange-flavored liqueur or orange juice
⅓ cup sugar
¼ cup butter

Citrus-Flavored Butter

½ cup butter, room temperature
¼ cup sugar
Grated peel of 1 orange
Grated peel of 1 lemon

In a medium bowl, combine flour and salt. Stir in eggs, milk, and ⅓ cup melted butter. Beat with a whisk until blended. Let stand 15 to 30 minutes. Heat a 6-inch crepe pan over medium-high heat. Grease pan with shortening. Pour about ¼ cup crepe batter into pan. Quickly swirl to cover bottom of pan, then immediately pour excess batter back into bowl. Cook until crepe is golden on bottom. Turn and cook 15 seconds or until sizzling stops. Stack cooked crepes on a sheet of waxed paper. Repeat until all crepes are cooked, adding shortening as needed. Prepare Citrus-Flavored Butter. To serve, spread each crepe with about 2 teaspoons Citrus-Flavored Butter; fold crepes in half, then in half again. Pour orange liqueur or orange juice into a heatproof serving pan or platter. Stir in sugar and ¼ cup butter. Place over medium heat until butter melts. Add folded crepes; keep warm. Makes about 15 crepes.

Citrus-Flavored Butter
In a small bowl, cream butter and sugar; blend in grated peels.

Scandinavian Game Buffet

HISTORICALLY, Scandinavians have included game birds in their diet. An old Swedish cookbook gives a recipe for "breast of crows braised with onions." Today, game birds are scarce and are a specialty dish.

We had the rare privilege of dining on breast of ptarmigan at the Pohjanhovi Restaurant in Rovaniemi, northern Finland. We had to place our order at least two weeks early so the chef could have fresh ptarmigan on hand. It was worth the wait. The ptarmigan had a delicate game flavor and was served in a rich, creamy sauce.

The traditional accompaniment for game birds is lingonberries, plain or sugared. Preserved lingonberries make an authentic substitute.

Pheasant, pigeon, ptarmigan, partridge, grouse, or woodcock are game birds that may be cooked in the same manner as the quail in the recipe here. Quail is available in many supermarkets and in large, well-stocked gourmet food stores in most countries. Lacking all of these, Cornish game hens or breasts or broiler-fryer chickens may be substituted. Of course, Cornish game hens and chicken will not have the same robust flavor as wild birds.

In northern Finland, reindeer often appears on restaurant menus. You have the choice of *käristys,* a stew-like mixture, or *paisti,* reindeer that is thinly sliced and quickly panfried with bacon. Smoked reindeer is a specialty that is often part of a smörgåsbord menu. Deer, elk, and reindeer are the principal game meats in Scandinavia.

Choose between Pan-Roasted Game Hens and Aquavit Hens for your main dish in this menu. The tomatoes and potatoes are simple and easy, but should be prepared just before serving. Prepare the soup and dessert ahead of time.

Spinach Soup

Spenatsoppa—Sweden

Scandinavians sometimes top this velvety soup with sour cream.

1 tablespoon butter
1 pound spinach or 1 package frozen spinach (10 ounces), thawed
¼ cup all-purpose flour
2 cups chicken broth
1 teaspoon salt
¼ teaspoon ground white pepper
¼ teaspoon ground allspice
2 cups milk
½ cup whipping cream

Melt butter in a medium saucepan over medium heat. Add spinach; stir until heated through. Stir in flour until moistened. Increase heat to high and slowly stir in chicken broth; cook and stir until thickened. Remove from heat and puree in a blender or food processor; pour puree into saucepan. Add salt, white pepper, allspice, milk, and cream. Stir over medium heat just until soup comes to a boil. Serve immediately. Makes 4 to 6 servings.

Pan-Roasted Game Hens

Ungstekt Vaktel—Sweden

Cover these tiny game birds so they don't overcook and become tough and dry.

4 quail, partridge, or wild pheasants
3 tablespoons butter
1 tablespoon lemon juice
3 tablespoons aquavit or brandy, if desired
4 slices white bread, toasted, buttered
1 teaspoon Dijon or Swedish-style mustard
2 tablespoons red currant jelly
¼ cup firm butter, cut in ½-inch cubes
1 to 2 tablespoons water, if necessary

Rinse hens; pat dry with paper towels. Using a heavy knife or poultry shears, split lengthwise unless very small. Melt 3 tablespoons butter in large, heavy skillet over medium heat. Add hens and lemon juice; brown slowly on all sides. Cover and cook 20 to 30 minutes or until hens are tender. Pour aquavit or brandy, if used, into a small metal measuring cup. Warm over low heat. Ignite and pour over cooked hens. Place 1 slice buttered toast on each of 4 dinner plates; top each with a cooked hen. Keep warm. Stirring vigorously with a whisk, boil pan drippings over high heat until reduced to a thick glaze. Whisk in mustard and jelly, then butter cubes, until melted and blended. If sauce separates, whisk in 1 to 2 tablespoons water. Spoon evenly over hens. Serve immediately. Makes 4 servings.

Aquavit Hens

Kokt Höns—Sweden

Swedes also cook duck, partridge, and grouse this way.

¼ cup butter
2 Cornish game hens (1 pound each), halved
1 cup dry white wine or chicken broth
1 teaspoon dried dill weed
½ teaspoon dried leaf thyme
½ to 1 teaspoon salt
2 tablespoons aquavit, brandy, or gin, if desired

Melt butter in large, heavy skillet over medium heat. Add game hens; brown on all sides. Pour wine or chicken broth over browned hens. Add dill, thyme, ½ teaspoon salt, and aquavit, brandy, or gin, if desired. Cover and simmer 20 to 30 minutes or until hens are tender. Place cooked hens on a plate; keep warm. Skim fat from drippings, then boil drippings until a thick glaze forms. Return hens to skillet; spoon glaze over hens. When hot, sprinkle with remaining ½ teaspoon salt, if desired. Arrange glazed hens on a medium platter. Spoon glaze from skillet over top. Serve immediately. Makes 4 servings.

Panned Cherry Tomatoes

Grillade Tomater—Sweden

Cherry tomatoes are a common garden vegetable in Scandinavia.

    3 tablespoons butter
    1 pint cherry tomatoes, stemmed, washed
    ½ teaspoon salt

Melt butter in large skillet over high heat. Add tomatoes; shake skillet so tomatoes roll around as they heat. Sauté 2 to 3 minutes or until tomatoes are heated through. Sprinkle with salt; serve immediately. Makes a pretty garnish for steaks, hamburger, and chicken. Makes 4 servings.

Creamy Fried Potatoes

Skåskpotatis—Sweden

Diced potatoes cook quickly in butter and are delicious served in cream.

4 large potatoes, peeled
1 medium onion
¼ cup butter
1 to 1½ cups water
¾ cup whipping cream
1 teaspoon salt
½ teaspoon freshly ground black pepper
¼ cup chopped fresh parsley

Cut potatoes into ½-inch dice; place in a bowl of ice water to prevent browning. Cut onion into ½-inch dice. Melt butter in a large skillet over high heat; add drained potatoes and onion. Shake pan frequently; sauté until potatoes are golden brown. Add 1 cup water; use a spoon to arrange potatoes and onion in an even layer. Cook, uncovered, over high heat until water evaporates, about 10 minutes. If potatoes are not tender, add remaining ½ cup water; boil until water evaporates. Pour cream evenly over cooked potatoes and onion; sprinkle with salt and pepper. Over medium heat, bring almost to a boil. Stirring gently, simmer 5 to 10 minutes or until cream is reduced in volume and thickened to a smooth sauce. Spoon mixture into a serving dish. Garnish with parsley. Serve hot. Makes 4 to 6 servings.

Grape Pudding

Krem—Norway

This favorite of young and old is light, refreshing, and simple to prepare.

½ cup quick-cooking tapioca
5 cups bottled grape juice
½ cup sugar
Pinch salt
Whipped cream, slightly sweetened

In a large saucepan, combine tapioca, grape juice, sugar, and salt. Stir to mix and let stand 15 minutes. Bring to a boil over high heat, stirring constantly. Reduce heat to low. Continue to stir and cook 15 minutes or until very thick. Cover and cool to room temperature. Pour into a serving bowl or individual dessert dishes. Serve at room temperature or refrigerate until chilled. Serve with slightly sweetened whipped cream. Makes 6 servings.

Midsummer's Day Buffet

MENU

Appetizer Platter

Butter, Variety of Breads

Salmon-in-a-Crust

Cottage Cheese Pastry

Horseradish Mayonnaise

Sliced Tomatoes and Cucumbers

Carrot-Apple Salad

Strawberry Cream Cake

Fruit-Juice Glögg, Milk, Coffee

BY MIDSUMMER'S DAY, spring fever has come to a head and summer is ready to blossom. June 24 is the longest day of the year in Scandinavia. In a large part of Scandinavia, the sun doesn't set—it just skims the horizon.

Some scholars believe the midsummer's festival is a continuation of the old pagan fire festival in honor of Balder, the sun god. Pious Christians tried in vain to end this heathen festival. They later changed the name of the celebration to honor St. John the Baptist. Now midsummer is known in Finland as *Juhannuspaivä*, in Sweden as *Johannes Dop,* in Denmark as *Sankt Hans,* and in Norway as *Johsok* or Sankt Hans.

In most places today, Midsummer's Day is celebrated by dancing around a maypole—a tall pole or mast bedecked with leaves and flowers that is ceremoniously raised. It is a time for dancing, feasting, picnics, and parties.

Midsummer's season is a perfect time to travel in Scandinavia. But it is best to check with the national tourist office of each country for a list of special celebrations.

An annual celebration is held in Helsinki, Finland, in the national folk museum park, *Seurasaari*. Here, colorfully costumed dancers, with flowers and ribbons streaming from their hair, demonstrate native dances. The setting is among transplanted historic country buildings. Girls dressed in national costumes sit on old-fashioned swings decorated with flowers. The maypole is decorated. There are bonfires, fiddlers, and accordion players. Demonstrators make all kinds of old-fashioned foods for the public to sample. Festivities start on Midsummer's Eve and continue through Midsummer's Day. It's a time for open-air parties, if the weather is good.

To transplant a bit of festivity to your area of the world, sponsor a cooperative smörgåsbord using the menu on page 177. Or use the menu above, which is not grandiose, but is full of delicious food ideas. The dishes can be prepared in advance. Salmon is traditional on most Midsummer's Day tables, perhaps because sport fishermen have been lucky. Even Salmon-in-a-Crust can be prepared ahead.

Appetizer Platter
Smörgåsplattar—Scandinavia

Add to or subtract from this mini-smörgåsbord as you wish.

2 sticks butter (½ cup each), room temperature
1 can sardines (3 ounces)
1 head Boston or butter lettuce
1 large, white sweet onion, sliced
1 large apple, sliced
1 European-style cucumber or other cucumber (8 inches), thinly sliced
¼ pound smoked herring, whitefish, salmon, or trout
½ to 1 pound Herrgardsost, spiced nökkelost, gjetost, Gorgonzola, Edam, Gouda or Swiss cheese, sliced
1 cup sliced radishes
½ pound bacon, cooked crisp
1 jar whitefish, lumpfish, or salmon caviar (2 ounces)
1 jar herring fillets in wine sauce (8 ounces)
Cardamom Crackers (page 110) or purchased crackers
Danish Pumpernickel (page 247), thinly sliced

Place butter on 2 butter trays or stir and spoon into a serving bowl. Place on serving table. On a large serving tray, arrange remaining appetizer items, leaving sardines, caviar, and herring in containers. Arrange crisp breads and pumpernickel in a basket or on a tray. Let guests serve themselves. Makes about 12 servings.

Salmon-in-a-Crust

Lohipiirakka—Finland

Every Finnish host has his or her own version of this fish pie.

2 pounds fresh or frozen salmon fillets
2 tablespoons butter
1 tablespoon lemon juice
1 teaspoon salt
2 tablespoons minced fresh parsley
1 tablespoon dried dill weed
Salt and pepper to taste
Cottage Cheese Pastry (page 154)
1½ cups cooked rice
¼ cup butter, melted
3 hard-cooked eggs, sliced
1 egg, thoroughly beaten
Melted butter
Lemon wedges for garnish
Horseradish Mayonnaise (page 155)

Thaw frozen salmon. Rinse fillets; wipe dry with paper towels. Melt 2 table-spoons butter in large skillet over high heat. Add salmon fillets; sauté 2½ minutes on each side. Sprinkle with lemon juice and 1 teaspoon salt. Trim cooked salmon fillets so they resemble the shape of a fish, 15 inches long and tapering from 5 to 3 inches wide. Set aside. In a small bowl, combine salmon trimmings, parsley, dill, and salt and pepper to taste. Refrigerate at least 20 minutes. Cover a large ungreased baking sheet with parchment paper, or grease a baking sheet; set aside. Prepare Cottage Cheese Pastry. On a lightly floured surface, roll out half of pastry to make an 18 x 8-inch oval. Shape one end to resemble a fish tail, not less than 6 inches wide. Arrange pastry on prepared baking sheet. Cut pieces of dough scraps to represent fins; press in place. Spread parsley mixture over pastry to within 2 inches of edge; top with rice. Drizzle with ¼ cup melted butter. Top with a layer of hard-cooked eggs. Cut salmon fillets in 4- or 5-inch pieces for easier handling. Top eggs with cooked salmon fillets. Roll remaining half of dough to a 20 x 10-inch oval. Moisten edges of bottom crust with water. Arrange top crust over salmon layer. Press top and bottom crusts together, pressing with the sides of your hands to seal. Trim, following lines of bottom crust, shaping fins and tail. Brush surface with beaten egg. Preheat oven to 375°F (190°C). Cut a hole where eye of fish should be. Insert a small ball of dough to keep hole open. With tips of scissor blades, cut top crust to simulate fish scales; these scales also serve as air vents during baking. Bake 35 minutes or until crust is lightly browned but still pale. To serve, cut in crosswise slices. Serve with melted butter, lemon wedges, and Horseradish Mayonnaise. Makes 8 servings.

Cottage Cheese Pastry

Rahkakuori—Finland

Use this lovely, flaky pastry for sweet or savory pies.

    1 cup (2 sticks) cold, firm butter
    2 cups all-purpose flour
    1 cup small-curd cottage cheese
    1 to 2 tablespoons ice water, if needed

In a large bowl, cut butter into flour until mixture is crumbly and pieces are about the size of peas. Stir in cottage cheese until mixture forms a crumbly dough. Knead lightly to shape into a ball, adding ice water a few drops at a time, if necessary. Chill 30 minutes before rolling out. Makes enough pastry for a 9-inch double-crust pie.

Horseradish Mayonnaise

Pepparrotsmajonnäs—Sweden

This is excellent with any cold fish.

½ cup whipping cream
1 cup mayonnaise
3 tablespoons grated fresh horseradish

In a medium bowl, beat cream until soft peaks form. Fold in mayonnaise and horseradish until blended. Refrigerate 15 to 30 minutes for flavors to blend. Makes about 2 cups.

Carrot-Apple Salad
Morot och Äpplesallad—Sweden

In Sweden, this salad is usually served with fish.

2 medium, tart apples
4 large carrots, peeled, shredded
1 tablespoon fresh lemon juice
Crisp lettuce leaves

Wash apples; cut in quarters and remove cores. Do not peel; cut in fine dice. In a large bowl, combine diced apples, carrots, and lemon juice. Refrigerate at least 20 minutes to chill. Arrange lettuce leaves on 8 individual salad plates or on a large platter. Spoon salad onto lettuce-lined plates or platter. Makes 8 servings.

Strawberry Cream Cake

Bløtekake—Norway

This is the most popular of the decorated cakes in Scandinavia.

⅓ cup all-purpose flour
¼ cup cornstarch
1 teaspoon baking powder
4 eggs, separated
¾ cup granulated sugar
Custard Filling (see below)
1 pint fresh strawberries
1½ cups whipping cream
2 tablespoons powdered sugar
1 teaspoon vanilla extract

Custard Filling
2 egg yolks, slightly beaten
1½ tablespoons butter
1 tablespoon cornstarch
1 cup half-and-half
2 tablespoons sugar
2 teaspoons vanilla extract

Butter a 9- or 10-inch springform pan; dust with flour; set aside. Preheat oven to 350°F (175°C). In a small bowl, combine flour, cornstarch, and baking powder. In a large bowl, beat egg whites until fluffy. Gradually beat in granulated sugar until stiff peaks form; set aside. In a small bowl, beat egg yolks until pale. Fold beaten egg yolks, and then flour mixture into beaten egg whites. Pour batter into prepared pan. Bake 30 minutes or until top of cake feels dry. Center of cake will be slightly indented. Let stand 5 minutes. Remove side of pan. Loosen cake from bottom of pan; cool cake on a rack. Prepare Custard Filling. Reserve 5 strawberries for top of cake. Slice remaining strawberries lengthwise; set aside. In a medium bowl, beat cream until stiff peaks form. Beat in powdered sugar and vanilla. When cake is cooled, cut horizontally into 3 thin layers. Place bottom layer on a cake platter; spread with half of Custard Filling and half of sliced strawberries. Place second cake layer on top. Spoon remaining Custard Filling and sliced strawberries over top. Place remaining cake layer on top. Spoon whipped-cream mixture over top of cake and decorate with reserved strawberries. Serve immediately or refrigerate until ready to serve. Makes 16 servings.

Custard Filling

In a small saucepan, blend egg yolks, butter, cornstarch, half-and-half, and sugar. Stirring constantly, cook over medium heat until smooth and thickened. Cover pan and set aside to cool. Stir vanilla into cooled custard.

Fruit-Juice Glögg

Saft Glögg—Sweden

This family-style glögg is popular in all of Scandinavia during Advent.

1 medium orange
8 cups apple cider
2 cups white grape juice or currant juice
¼ cup sugar
1 cinnamon stick (3 inches)
8 whole cloves
⅔ cup raisins
⅔ cup slivered blanched almonds

Using a vegetable peeler, cut colored portion from orange in a single spiral. Reserve orange for another purpose. In a large pot, combine orange peel and remaining ingredients. Let stand 4 hours. Bring to a boil over medium heat. Reduce heat to low; simmer 30 minutes. Serve hot or cold in punch cups, including some raisins and almonds in each serving. Makes 12 servings.

Karelian Country-Style Dinner

MENU

Karelian Ragout

Baked Wild Rice

Leaf Lettuce Salad

Karelian Pies

Egg Butter, Fruit Pudding

Beer, Mineral Water, Milk, Buttermilk, Coffee

THE FOOD OF FINLAND has more diversity than any other Scandinavian country. This is because Finland is a buffer zone between East and West. It shares a western border with Sweden and Norway and an eastern border with Russia.

Foods of western Finland reflect strong similarities with the rest of Scandinavia. In the east, the folk arts, handicrafts, poetry, music, and food of Karelia have woven a special richness into Finnish life. The Finnish national epic, the *Kalevala,* and the Finnish national instrument, the *Kantele,* come from Karelia.

After the eastern part of Karelia was lost to Russia in 1939 and 1940, many of the people moved west and were welcomed into the homes of other Finns. Property was divided. Finns shared their wealth to help relocate and resettle the Karelians. People donated jewelry, money, or whatever they had. A great aunt of ours, admiring my wedding rings, glanced at her left hand and remarked, "Yes, I had rings once, but I donated them to the Karelian cause."

Karelian cooking depends on the abundant use of the oven. This was a main point of friction between the "two women of the house." In western Finland, in the spring and fall, it was the custom to bake round, flat, rye bread with a hole in the center. The loaves were strung on poles and hung in the *aitta,* or grainery, to dry. This preserved them for the coming season. Karelians, on the other hand, baked their fat, round, sour-rye loaves every day. Karelians complained that the Finnish sour-rye bread was so tough it broke their teeth. The western Finns complained that the Karelians baked so much it cracked their ovens!

Because the oven was always hot, Karelians made *piirakka,* or meat pies. The most popular piirakka is a rice filling baked in a rye crust. Today Karelian piirakka are available in almost every supermarket, bakery, delicatessen, and coffee shop in Finland. Finns use them as popular lunchbox sandwiches. Restaurants serve piirakka as a base for *smørrebrød* sandwiches.

Karelian Ragout

Karjalan Paisti—Finland

In olden days, this was made from trimmings after the fall butchering.

> 1 pound lean stewing beef
> 1 pound lean, boneless stewing lamb
> 1 pound lean pork shoulder
> 1 medium onion, sliced
> 1 tablespoon salt
> 6 whole allspice
> 1 bay leaf, crumbled
> 1 can whole small onions (16 ounces), drained
> 8 ounces fresh, whole, small mushrooms
> Boiled whole potatoes or cooked wild rice

Trim fat from meat before weighing. Cut meat into 1-inch cubes. Preheat oven to 250°F (120°C). Separate sliced onion into rings. Layer meat and onion rings in a heavy 3-quart oven-to-table casserole dish, sprinkling each layer with salt. Top with allspice and bay leaf. Cover with a tight-fitting lid. Bake 3 hours; stir. Bake 3 hours longer or until meat is tender. Spoon canned onions and fresh mushrooms over meat mixture. Bake 15 minutes, uncovered. Spoon some of broth that has formed over potatoes or wild rice. Makes 8 servings.

Baked Wild Rice

Minnesota Villiriisi—Finnish Americans

Bake this simple wild rice dish in the oven with Karelian Ragout (page 162).

  1 cup wild rice, uncooked
  4 cups beef or chicken broth
  1 teaspoon salt
  ½ teaspoon pepper
  1 tablespoon butter

Preheat oven to 250°F (120°C). Wash wild rice in 3 changes of hot tap water. In a heavy 2-quart casserole dish, combine washed rice, broth, salt, pepper, and butter. Cover and bake 3 hours. Fluff rice with a fork. Makes 8 servings.

Leaf Lettuce Salad

Lehtisalaatti—Finland

The simple lemon-cream dressing is especially good with fresh garden lettuce.

2 quarts garden leaf lettuce or other salad greens, or about 2 medium
   heads, washed, dried
¼ cup fresh lemon juice
1 tablespoon sugar
½ teaspoon salt
Dash freshly ground black pepper
¼ cup whipping cream

Tear lettuce greens in 1- to 2-inch pieces. Place in a salad bowl; refrigerate.
Combine lemon juice, sugar, salt, and pepper in a small bowl. Beat with
a whisk while slowly adding cream. Continue beating until blended and
creamy. Drizzle dressing over lettuce; toss to distribute. Serve immediately.
Makes 6 to 8 servings.

Karelian Pies

Karjalan Piirakka—Finland

These oval shaped pies in a rye crust reveal the rice filling through the top.

1 cup medium-grain rice, uncooked
1 cup water
About 3 cups milk
2 tablespoons butter
2 to 3 teaspoons salt
½ cup butter
½ cup milk
Rye Crust (see below)
Egg Butter (page 167)

Rye Crust

1 cup water
2 tablespoons butter, melted
1 teaspoon salt
1½ cups all-purpose flour
1½ cups rye flour

In a medium saucepan, bring rice and water to a boil over high heat. Stir in 3 cups milk. Reduce heat to low; cover and cook until rice is tender, 20 to 25 minutes. Add 2 tablespoons butter and salt to taste. Beat with a wooden spoon until mixture is creamy. Add more milk, if necessary, until consistency is similar to cooked oatmeal. Set aside to cool. Grease 3 or 4 baking sheets or cover with parchment paper; set aside. Prepare a glaze by melting ½ cup butter in a small saucepan over low heat; stir in ½ cup milk. Heat until milk is hot, stirring occasionally; set aside and keep warm. Prepare Rye Crust. Spread ¼ cup cooked rice filling on each dough circle to within 1 inch of edge. Fold uncovered edge of dough over filling, making a boat-shape oval, narrower and sharply pointed on two opposite ends. Leaving center open, crimp crust edge in even *pleats* as it is brought up over filling. Place pies, 2 to 3 inches apart, on prepared baking sheets. Preheat oven to 450°F (230°C). Brush pies with warm butter-and-milk glaze. Bake glazed pies 15 minutes. Brush with glaze after 7 minutes and again after removing from oven. Serve hot or cold with Egg Butter. Makes 16 pies.

Rye Crust

In a large bowl, combine water, butter, salt, and all-purpose flour; beat until smooth. Stir in rye flour to make a stiff dough similar to a yeast dough. Turn out onto board dusted with rye flour. Knead until smooth, about 5 minutes. Divide into 4 equal pieces. Cut each piece into fourths. Shape each piece into a ball. On lightly floured board, roll out each ball of dough into a 6-inch circle.

Egg Butter
Munavoi—Finland

Use this spread on Karelian Pies (page 165), rye bread, sandwiches, or toast.

    1 cup butter, room temperature
    ¼ teaspoon salt
    ⅛ teaspoon ground ginger
    4 hard-cooked eggs, finely chopped

In a medium bowl, beat butter, salt, and ginger until light and fluffy. Stir in eggs. Serve immediately or store in refrigerator. Serve at room temperature. Makes 2 cups.

Fruit Pudding
Marja Kiiseli—Finland

This dessert can be prepared in advance, and is good either hot or cold.

4 cups water
3 cups fresh or frozen blueberries, raspberries, boysenberries,
    strawberries, or blackberries
½ cup sugar
3 tablespoons cornstarch
Whipping cream

In a large saucepan, combine water and berries. Bring to a boil over medium heat, stirring to break up frozen fruit. In a small bowl, combine sugar and cornstarch. Slowly add to boiling fruit mixture while whisking vigorously. Stir and cook until thickened, about 15 minutes. If undercooked, mixture may break down and become thin after cooling. Serve hot or cold. To serve, pour cream over individual servings. Makes 8 servings.

Dinner in Finnish Lake Country

MENU

Iron Range Fish Stew

Fish Pâté

Melted Butter and Lemon Wedges

Finnish Cucumber Salad

Strawberries and Cream or

Finnish Air Pudding (page 219)

Beer, Milk, Buttermilk, Coffee, Tea

ONE OF THE MOST SCENIC AREAS OF FINLAND is found northeast of Helsinki, in the Saimaa Lake District. Travelers take a short train ride from Helsinki to the village of Lapeenranta. Here they board a comfortable Finnish steamer, which travels along a scenic northern route to Kuopio, a village situated in Karelia District. The trip takes you along pine-rimmed lakes very near the border of Russia.

In Kuopio, you can visit a colorful open market and purchase one of the world's most unique foods, a fish pie or *kalakukko*. Kalakukko is made fresh every day by homebakers and sold in the market, still warm from the oven. Exotic in its unusual flavor, kalakukko is simple to make with tiny, bony, fresh-water fish called *muikku*, a relative of herring. Baked long and slowly, the bones soften so they melt in your mouth.

Kalakukko look like plump, round loaves of rye bread. The thick rye crust acts almost as a casserole dish enclosing the filling. Finns make other *kukko* versions filled with beef chunks and potatoes or pork and turnips. The fish filling is the local favorite for picnics, lunches, or snacks.

169

In our recipe, Kalakukko, or Fish Pâté, is made with pike or perch because of their availability. To serve this pâté, slice it like a loaf of bread, or cut a slice off the top of the loaf and scoop out the savory filling. Break off pieces of the delicious rye crust to eat with the filling.

Iron Range Fish Stew

Kalamojakka—Finnish Americans

The term mojakka *means fish stew to American Finns—no one knows its origin.*

   3 pounds fresh or frozen freshwater trout, walleye, or whitefish fillets
   6 large potatoes, peeled, cut in large cubes
   1 large onion, diced
   2 teaspoons salt
   5 whole allspice
   6 cups water
   2 cups whipping cream or 1 can evaporated milk (13 ounces)
   2 tablespoons butter
   ¼ teaspoon dried dill weed, if desired

Thaw frozen fish. Remove skin and bones, if necessary; set aside. In a large pot or soup kettle, combine potatoes, onion, salt, allspice, and water. Cover and bring to a boil over medium heat. Reduce heat to low; simmer until potatoes are tender, 15 to 20 minutes. Cut fish in 2-inch pieces. Use a slotted spoon to add fish pieces to stew. Cover and simmer 15 minutes longer or until fish flakes easily. Do not boil. Fish will remain in pieces. Stir in whipping cream or evaporated milk, butter, and dill, if desired. Serve hot. Makes 6 servings.

Fish Pâté

Kalakukko—Finland

This bacon-flavored fish pie tastes best when served warm.

1½ pounds small pike, perch, or trout, fresh or frozen
Rye Crust (see below)
1 teaspoon salt
½ pound sliced bacon
½ cup butter
½ cup water
Melted butter
Lemon wedges

Rye Crust

4 cups stirred rye flour
½ to 1 cup all-purpose flour
2 teaspoons salt
2 cups warm water
2 tablespoons butter, melted

Thaw frozen fish. Clean fish, removing entrails, head, tail, and scales. It is not necessary to remove skin and bones. Prepare Rye Crust. Stack half of fish onto center of dough, leaving 4 inches on all sides uncovered. Sprinkle with ½ teaspoon salt. Top with bacon. Add remaining fish and salt. Fold sides of dough to center, over filling. Moisten edges slightly with water; pinch edges to seal. Preheat oven to 300°F (150°C). To prepare glaze, heat butter and water in a small saucepan over medium heat until butter melts. Grease a large baking sheet with raised sides. Place filled crust on center of baking sheet. Brush surface of pie with butter-and-water glaze. Make a 1½-inch slash in top of crust. Bake 1½ hours, brushing occasionally with glaze. Cut a piece of foil large enough to enclose pie. Place baked pie on foil; wrap airtight. Return wrapped pie to baking sheet; bake 3 hours longer. Turn off oven; leave pie in oven 2 hours longer or until oven has cooled. This will soften crust. To serve, slice crosswise, or cut a 3-inch oval in the top of the crust. Scoop out filling. Serve hot, warm, or cold. Spoon melted butter over filling, followed by lemon juice squeezed from wedges. Break off pieces of crust to serve with filling. Makes 4 dinner servings or 8 snack or appetizer servings.

Rye Crust

In a large bowl, combine rye flour, ¼ cup all-purpose flour, and salt. Stir in water, then butter. Add enough all-purpose flour to make a stiff dough. Turn out onto a board lightly sprinkled with rye flour. Knead dough until smooth. Dough will feel similar to clay. Roll out dough to a 14-inch square, about ½ inch thick.

Finnish Cucumber Salad

Kurkkusalaatti—Finland

Thin slicing lets the marinade penetrate the cucumbers, making them crisp and tangy.

    1 European-style cucumber (10 to 12 inches) or 2 smaller cucumbers
      (6 inches)
    2 tablespoons dried dill weed
    ½ cup distilled white vinegar
    ½ cup sugar
    ¼ cup water
    1 teaspoon salt

Cut cucumber in paper-thin slices. In a medium bowl, layer sliced cucumbers, sprinkling dill between layers. In a small bowl, combine vinegar, sugar, water, and salt. Pour over cucumber mixture. Refrigerate 4 to 5 hours. Makes 4 to 6 servings.

❀Smörgåsbords

Cooperative Smörgåsbord

MENU

———

FIRST COURSE:

Glass-Master's Herring

Mustard Herring (page 82)

COLD FOOD COURSE:

Swedish Beef Tongue

Pressed-Pork Roll (page 84)

Danish Cucumber Salad

Danish Curry Salad

Pineapple-Beet Salad

HOT FOOD COURSE:

Fish Frikadeller

Jansson's Temptation

Karelian Ragout (page 162)

Rutabaga-Potato Casserole (page 216)

Flatbreads, Swedish Limpa (page 248)

Bond Ost, Gammelost, Jarlsberg Cheeses

Smoked Farmer's Cheese

DESSERT COURSE:

Cranberry-Rye Pudding

Chocolate-Dipped Orange Sticks (page 284)

Red or White Wine, Coffee, Tea

———————

 SMÖRGÅSBORD IS NOT LIMITED TO SWEDISH celebrations. In Finland, it is called *voileipäpöytä*. Both words translate to *bread-and-butter table*. In Norway and Denmark it is called *koltbord,* which means *cold table*. They all mean that the food served will be delicious with, or on, bread and butter.

Originally, a smörgåsbord was a community effort. According to legend, the horse and buggy ride to church on Sunday was a long one. Church services were not short, and people became very hungry. Families began bringing food to share—each woman bringing her specialty. Thus the smörgåsbord was born.

The smörgåsbord in modern Scandinavia follows the same menu pattern established years ago. Breads and butter are placed at the head of the table. They are followed by a selection of pickled and preserved herring, cold fish and meats, salads, and cooked potatoes. Plain boiled potatoes are part of every course but dessert. Next the hot foods are served. Cheese, cold puddings, and desserts come last.

There is a definite pattern to serving oneself at a smörgåsbord. Food is never heaped on a plate. The idea is to sample the foods a few at a time, making several trips to the table. This keeps the various flavors of foods separate and distinct.

The first course of the meal is always bread and herring. When you return to the table for the next course, take a clean plate. This time, sample the cold smoked and salted fish combinations and cold meats. For the third course, take another clean plate and sample the hot foods. Next, taking another clean plate, sample the salads, cheese, and hot and cold vegetable dishes. As a climax to the meal, take another clean plate and sample the desserts or the cheese and fruits. Coffee is served after dessert.

Serve your smörgåsbord on a round, square, or oblong table large enough to hold all of the food without crowding. If the wood grain is pretty, the table may be left bare. Depending on the mood you want to convey, leave the table bare or cover it with a rough woven or fine linen cloth. Place the food so the normal flow of traffic will take your guests from the first course to the last. By placing the plates, silverware, bread, and cold fish dishes together, your guests will know where to start.

Scandinavians use natural table decorations. You will never see artificial flowers on a table in Scandinavia. In the spring, the table may be decorated with sprouted branches of bushes or trees, or with a basket of pretty Easter eggs nestled in fresh foliage. In the summer, they often use a small bucket of fresh wild flowers. At one home, a lovely glass bowl was filled with water and colorful rocks from the seashore. At another, for a Christmas celebration, a small pine tree was set in a tall candle holder and decorated with candles. Candles are often used on the table. In Scandinavia, you can purchase candles in every color of the spectrum.

In Scandinavia, you seldom see a full smörgåsbord in a home. However, you may see an abbreviated version or *smörgåsplatter,* which makes a fine first course to a meal. To prepare all the dishes for a full smörgåsbord by yourself is a monumental task. It is better to follow the traditional pattern and invite others to a cooperative smörgåsbord. If this is not possible, have part or all of the meal catered by a hotel, restaurant, or gourmet shop.

The menu that follows contains more dishes than could possibly be used at a single smörgåsbord. Select and prepare two or more items from each of the courses, with particular attention to creating a variety of ingredients, color, and flavor. *Skol!* Or as the Finns say, *Kippis!*

Glass-Master's Herring
Glasmästarsill—Swedish

The name comes from the procedure of layering herring and spices in a glass jar.

> 1 jar herring fillets in wine sauce (16 ounces)
> 1 teaspoon whole allspice, crushed
> 1 tablespoon pickling spices
> 1½ tablespoons shredded fresh gingerroot
> ½ teaspoon mustard seeds
> ¼ cup diced fresh horseradish
> 2 red onions, thinly sliced
> 1 small carrot, peeled, thinly sliced
> ½ cup sugar
> ¾ cup distilled white vinegar

Drain herring and discard juices. In a small bowl, combine allspice, pickling spices, gingerroot, mustard seeds, and horseradish. In a deep glass bowl or jar, layer half of the sliced onion and half of the carrot. Add all of drained herring. Sprinkle spice mixture over herring. Top with remaining onions and carrot. In a small bowl, combine sugar and vinegar. Pour over herring mixture. Cover and marinate in refrigerator for 3 days. Serve from marinade bowl or jar. Makes about 16 herring pieces.

To increase servings, double amount of herring without doubling remaining ingredients.

Swedish Beef Tongue

Oxtunga—Sweden

Serve this cold and thinly sliced, with mustard or a mustard sauce.

1 beef tongue (3 pounds)
1 onion, quartered
2 carrots, sliced
2 tablespoons mixed pickling spices
Water to cover

Scrub tongue under running water. Place tongue in a deep kettle; add onion, carrots, pickling spices, and water to cover. Bring to a boil, then simmer 3 to 3½ hours over low heat until tongue is tender when pierced with a fork. Cool in broth. Peel skin from tongue; cut away small bones and fatty portions. Refrigerate until ready to use. Strain broth; discard vegetables and spices. Reserve broth for sauces or soup. To serve tongue, slice thinly and arrange on a platter. Makes 20 to 24 appetizer servings.

Danish Cucumber Salad
Agurkesalat—Denmark

The marinade gives these crisp, paper-thin cucumber slices a sweet-sour flavor.

    1 European-style cucumber (16 inches) or 2 smaller cucumbers (8 inches)
    1 cup water
    1 cup distilled white vinegar
    ¼ teaspoon ground white pepper
    ¼ teaspoon salt
    1 cup sugar

Cut cucumbers in paper-thin slices, making about 4 cups. In a large bowl, combine remaining ingredients; stir until sugar dissolves. Stir in cucumbers. Refrigerate 4 to 6 hours. Drain. Serve marinated cucumbers in a pretty glass bowl. Makes 6 to 8 servings.

Danish Curry Salad

Karrysalat—Denmark

Curry is often used in Danish and Norwegian cuisine.

Curry Dressing (see below)
2 hard-cooked eggs, diced
1 jar herring in wine sauce (16 ounces), drained, chopped
1 cup chopped cooked ham
½ cup diced cucumber
2 cups cold cooked rice
Crisp lettuce leaves
Fresh fennel for garnish, if desired

Curry Dressing
¼ cup whipping cream
½ cup mayonnaise or salad dressing
1½ teaspoons curry powder
⅛ teaspoon salt
⅛ teaspoon ground white pepper
1 teaspoon white or red wine vinegar

Prepare Curry Dressing. In a large bowl, toss together eggs, herring, ham, cucumber, and rice. Fold in dressing. Line salad bowl or platter with lettuce leaves. Spoon salad onto lettuce. Garnish with fennel, if desired. Makes 6 servings.

Curry Dressing
In a medium bowl, whip cream until soft peaks form. Fold in remaining ingredients.

Pineapple-Beet Salad

Ananas Punajuurisalaatti—Finland

Fast and easy to prepare.

      1 can pineapple chunks (20 ounces), drained
      1 can pickled beets (16 ounces), drained and cut in julienne strips
      2 tablespoons white wine vinegar
      ¼ cup vegetable oil
      3 tablespoons sugar
      ½ teaspoon salt
      Dash ground white pepper
      Sprig of mint or 1 bay leaf for garnish

In a medium serving bowl, lightly toss pineapple and beets. In a small bowl, use a whisk to beat vinegar, oil, sugar, salt, and white pepper. Pour dressing over beets and pineapple; toss. Garnish with mint or bay leaf; serve immediately. Makes 6 to 8 servings.

Fish Frikadeller

Fiskefrikadeller—Denmark

"Frikadeller" is almost a synonym for Danish meatballs.

1 pound fresh or frozen cod or whitefish fillets
1 small onion, quartered
1 teaspoon salt
½ cup all-purpose flour
1 egg
⅛ teaspoon ground white pepper
½ teaspoon baking powder
1 cup milk
1 teaspoon curry powder, if desired
Butter for frying

Thaw frozen fish. Pat dry with paper towels. Skin and bone fish if necessary; cut fish into several pieces. Grind fish and onion in a food grinder 3 times or until pureed. In a large bowl, combine pureed fish mixture, salt, flour, egg, white pepper, baking powder, ½ cup milk, and curry powder, if desired. Beat until blended. If preferred, puree the fish using a food processor fitted with a steel blade. Turn processor on and drop in fish strips. Process until pureed, then add onion and process until minced. Add salt, flour, egg, white pepper, baking powder, ½ cup milk, and curry powder, if desired. Process until smooth. Spoon mixture into a large bowl. Place bowl over another large bowl filled with crushed ice. Chill, stirring, until mixture thickens. Slowly stir in remaining milk. Cover and chill over ice 20 minutes longer. In a large skillet over medium-low heat, melt enough butter to coat bottom of skillet. Dip 2 tablespoons into ice water until cold. Use cold spoons to shape fish mixture into egg-shape ovals. Fry ovals in butter 4 to 5 minutes on each side. Add more butter as needed. Serve hot. Makes 4 main dish servings, or about 20 fishballs.

Jansson's Temptation

Janssons Frestelse—Sweden

Serve this irresistible anchovy-and-potato casserole as a side dish or a midnight snack.

3 tablespoons butter
2 large onions, sliced
4 medium potatoes, peeled, cut in julienne strips
1 can Swedish anchovy fillets (3 ounces)
1 cup half-and-half

Butter a shallow 2-quart baking dish; set aside. Preheat oven to 400°F (205°C). Melt 1 tablespoon butter in a large skillet. Add onions; sauté 2 minutes or until soft but not browned, stirring occasionally. In a prepared baking dish, alternately layer potatoes, sautéed onions, and anchovies, beginning and ending with potatoes. Sprinkle 1 tablespoon of brine from anchovies over top. Dot with remaining 2 tablespoons butter. Pour ½ cup half-and-half over top. Cover and bake 25 minutes. Remove cover; add remaining half-and-half. Bake 25 minutes longer. Serve hot or at room temperature. Makes 6 servings.

Smoked Farmer's Cheese
Rygeost—Denmark

In Denmark, this caraway-flavored cheese is smoked over a nettle fire.

8 cups dairy buttermilk
½ cup whipping cream
½ to 1 teaspoon salt
2 tablespoons caraway seeds
Fresh fruit or vegetables

Preheat oven to 200°F (95°C). Pour buttermilk and cream into a 3- or 4-quart casserole dish. Cover and bake 2½ hours or until curds separate from whey. Line a colander or strainer with a damp towel or several layers of damp cheesecloth. Pour mixture through lined colander or strainer. Press to squeeze out as much liquid as possible. Let drain 2 hours. Spoon cheese into a medium bowl. Stir in salt to taste. Rinse out towel or cheesecloth and use to line colander or strainer again. Turn salted mixture into cheesecloth; place over a large bowl. Refrigerate and let drain overnight. Remove cheese from cloth; shape into a ball. Press caraway seeds onto surface of cheese. Place cheese ball in a large metal strainer. Place over a smoking charcoal fire, 10 minutes or until cheese is lightly coated from smoke. Do not burn. Serve immediately or refrigerate until chilled. Serve with fruit or vegetables. Makes about ½ pound cheese.

Cranberry-Rye Pudding

Ruismarjapuuro—Finland

Finns also like to serve this hot, for breakfast, with a little cream poured over the top.

1 cup rye flour
2 tablespoons cornstarch
½ cup sugar
½ teaspoon salt
4 cups cranberry juice
¼ cup dark corn syrup
2 tablespoons sugar
Sweetened whipped cream

In a large saucepan, combine rye flour, cornstarch, ½ cup sugar, and salt. Stir in cranberry juice and corn syrup. Beat with a whisk until blended. Stirring constantly with whisk, bring to a boil over medium heat. Cook until thickened, stirring occasionally, about 20 minutes. Place over a bowl of ice water. Stir with whisk until cool, about 10 minutes. Pour into a serving bowl. Sprinkle 2 tablespoons sugar over top. Cover and refrigerate. Serve with whipped cream. Makes 8 servings.

New Year's Eve Smörgåsbord

MENU

FIRST COURSE:

Sherried Herring, Mustard-Dill Mayonnaise

COLD FOOD COURSE:

Caviar-Stuffed Eggs

Pressed-Beef Roll (page 83)

Herring Salad, Dilled Potato Salad

Seafood-Grapefruit Mold

HOT FOOD COURSE:

Fish Mousse (page 104), Shrimp Sauce (page 106)

Smörgåsbord Meatballs

Apple-Stuffed Pork Loin

Cooked Whole Potatoes

Rye-Meal Bread (page 246)

White Potato Bread (page 239)

Havarti, Gammelost, Ekte Gjetost Cheeses

Finnish Egg Cheese

DESSERT COURSE:

Danish Rum Pudding, Raspberry Sauce

Finnish Rice Pudding (page 76)

Almond-Caramel Cake (page 223)

Fruit-Juice Glögg (page 159)

Hot Wine Punch

———————

MANY OLD SUPERSTITIONS AND BELIEFS are connected with New Year's Eve in Scandinavia. Some still feel that herring eaten on this night will bring good fortune. And if you eat cabbage or sauerkraut, an apple, or a bun and a piece of sausage, it will bring good health. Eaten together, this combination promises a good year. Red candles in the candelabra further assure good fortune.

In years past, farmers thought if their cows were in good spirits at the beginning of the new year, they would be fruitful during the year. Fruit trees were given an additional winter wrapping to assure a good crop. In reality, the wrapping may have protected the trees from hungry rabbits. Because of the deep snow, by New Year's the rabbits had a firm footing from which to reach the bark of the tree at a higher level.

It was considered risky to have cracked jars and jugs in the house. As midnight approached, all cracked jars and jugs were broken. It was also believed that the louder the noise made on New Year's, the farther away evil spirits would stay. Therefore, firecrackers were set off and there was much dancing and singing.

Scandinavians also believed that whatever happened on New Year's Day foretold what would happen during the year. Consequently, households were peaceful. People tried not to part with money. In fact, they tried to obtain money. Often an employee gave his employer a penny to wish him good profits for the coming year.

New Year's Eve, until about 1900, was a time for exchanging small gifts. This was an expression of the wish that the receiver would lack nothing during the coming year.

Today, many families spend New Year's Eve at home telling stories and predicting fortunes. Or, if there are parties, they often include whole families. One popular tradition is to melt small pieces of lead or tin in a heavy iron spoon in the fireplace. The molten metal is poured into a bucket of cold water, making it harden into an unusual shape. The piece is studied. Its shadow is cast on a wall and analyzed. Then an older member of the group or a soothsayer friend predicts fortunes for the coming year based on the object's shape and shadow. Fortunes are usually good, causing great excitement among the children.

All Scandinavian countries share the Christmas and New Year's tradition of serving a rice pudding dessert. A single almond is hidden in the pudding. The person finding the almond will enjoy good luck and has the privilege of handing out gifts, or they receive some other special award. Recently, at a Finnish language-and-culture camp in the United States, 85 campers were told about rice pudding and the significance of the almond. The pudding was served that night. The lucky person was to sing before the entire group. The cook buried an almond in 85 servings. The planners thought there would be a chorus, but not one person admitted finding the almond.

Sherried Herring

Sherrysill—Sweden

The flavor of sherry with herring makes this a delightful dish.

2 salted herring (about 1½ pounds)
½ cup sherry
¼ cup water
¼ cup white wine vinegar
½ cup sugar
¼ teaspoon ground allspice
2 onions, thinly sliced
Chopped fresh dill for garnish

In refrigerator, soak herring overnight in cold water to cover. Drain. Remove head, tail, skin, and backbone from fish. Rinse in cold water. Cut herring crosswise into ¾-inch slices. Place in a medium, nonmetal bowl. Combine sherry, water, vinegar, sugar, and allspice. Pour over fish. Top with onions. Cover and refrigerate 24 hours. Drain marinade off herring. Arrange herring and onion rings on a plate; garnish with dill. Makes about 24 herring pieces.

Mustard-Dill Mayonnaise

Laxsas—Scandinavia

Serve this sauce with Gravlax (Salted Salmon, page 209) or another hot or cold fish.

¼ cup Dijon mustard
1 teaspoon dry mustard
3 tablespoons sugar
2 tablespoons white wine vinegar
⅓ cup vegetable oil
3 tablespoons minced fresh dill

In a small, deep bowl, combine Dijon and dry mustard; blend in sugar and vinegar to make a paste. Whisk in oil until mixture resembles thick mayonnaise. Stir in dill. Let sauce stand at room temperature 25 minutes to let flavors blend. Makes 1 cup.

Caviar-Stuffed Eggs

Farserede Æg—Denmark

These are especially pretty when you use both red and black caviar to top the eggs.

    4 hard-cooked eggs
    1 tablespoon butter, room temperature
    1 tablespoon Dijon mustard
    3 tablespoons red or black caviar
    Parsley for garnish

Cut eggs in half lengthwise. Carefully remove egg yolks and place in a small bowl. Use a fork to mash egg yolks and blend in butter and mustard. Press through a small strainer to make smooth. Arrange egg whites, cut-side up, on a platter. Spoon egg-yolk mixture into centers of egg whites. Top each with about 1 teaspoon caviar; garnish with parsley. Makes 8 servings.

Herring Salad
Rosolli—Finland

Almost always found on a smörgåsbord menu, this makes an excellent salad for any meal.

2 cups diced, cooked beets or 1 can diced beets (16 ounces)
2 medium potatoes, peeled, cooked, diced
2 tart apples, peeled, diced
2 carrots, peeled, diced, cooked
1 small onion, minced
1 dill pickle, diced
1 cup diced pickled herring
Whipped Cream Dressing (see below)

Whipped Cream Dressing
1 cup whipping cream
2 tablespoons lemon juice
2 teaspoons beet juice
¼ teaspoon salt
Sugar to taste

Drain beets, reserving 2 teaspoons juice for dressing. In a large, shallow, serving bowl, arrange potatoes, apples, carrots, onion, pickle, and drained beets, side by side in rows. Arrange herring around edge of salad. Prepare Whipped Cream Dressing. Let guests serve themselves, mixing ingredients on their plates. Serve dressing with salad. Makes 8 dinner servings or 16 to 20 appetizer servings.

Whipped Cream Dressing
In a medium bowl, beat cream until soft peaks form. Fold in remaining ingredients. Spoon into a small serving bowl. Makes about 1 cup.

Dilled Potato Salad

Potatissallad—Scandinavia

A natural for the smörgåsbord and for picnics.

>   Dill Dressing (see below)
>   6 medium potatoes, peeled, cooked, chilled, sliced
>   2 tablespoons chopped green onion
>   2 tablespoons chopped fresh parsley
>   ½ cup diced pickled beets
>   2 tablespoons chopped chives or green onion tops

Dill Dressing

>   2 tablespoons white wine vinegar
>   1 teaspoon salt
>   ¼ teaspoon ground white pepper
>   ¼ teaspoon dried dill weed or to taste
>   6 tablespoons vegetable oil

Prepare Dill Dressing; set aside. In a large bowl, combine potatoes, green onion, parsley, beets, and chives or green onion tops. Pour dressing over potato mixture; toss to distribute. Refrigerate 30 minutes or until ready to serve. Makes 6 servings.

Dill Dressing

In a small bowl, combine all ingredients. Beat with a whisk until blended.

Seafood-Grapefruit Mold

Grapefrugt med Krabbe—Denmark

Tangy grapefruit flavors the gelatin ring and blends with an elegant crab salad filling.

1 can grapefruit segments (16 ounces)
1 envelope unflavored gelatin (¼ ounce)
About 1 cup white wine
¼ cup whipping cream
¼ cup mayonnaise
½ pound cooked crabmeat, drained
1 package frozen asparagus pieces, cooked, drained (10 ounces)
Lettuce leaves or parsley for garnish

Drain grapefruit, reserving juice in a 2-cup glass measure. Add gelatin to juice; soak 5 minutes. Place over pan of boiling water; stir until gelatin is dissolved. Add white wine to make 2 cups. Place over ice water; chill, stirring, until mixture has consistency of unbeaten egg whites. Pour ¼ cup mixture into bottom of a 3-cup ring mold. Refrigerate until set, about 20 minutes. Arrange drained grapefruit segments over top; cover with remaining partially set gelatin mixture. Refrigerate until set, about 2 hours. In a medium bowl, beat cream until stiff peaks form; fold in mayonnaise, then crabmeat and asparagus. Invert molded gelatin onto a serving plate; spoon crab salad into center. Garnish with lettuce leaves or parsley. Makes about 6 luncheon servings.

Smörgåsbord Meatballs

Små Köttbullar—Swedish

Meatballs for the smörgåsbord should be about the size of large marbles.

1 tablespoon butter
1 tablespoon minced onion
⅔ cup soft breadcrumbs
1 cup water
¾ pound lean ground beef
¼ pound lean ground pork
1 teaspoon salt
½ teaspoon ground allspice, if desired
½ teaspoon ground white pepper
½ teaspoon sugar
Butter for frying, melted
1 cup condensed beef consommé

Melt 1 tablespoon butter in a large skillet. Add onion; sauté 1 to 2 minutes until tender. In large bowl of electric mixer, combine breadcrumbs and water; let stand 1 to 2 minutes. Add beef, pork, sautéed onion, salt, allspice if desired, white pepper, and sugar. Beat with electric mixer on low speed until smooth. Turn mixer to high speed. Beat meat mixture until light and fluffy, about 10 minutes. Meat will lighten in color during beating. Dip 2 teaspoons in ice water until cold. Use cold spoons to shape meat into tiny meatballs. Pour melted butter for frying ¼ inch deep in a large skillet. Place over medium heat. Add meatballs to hot butter. Brown on all sides, constantly shaking pan. Drain on paper towels; keep warm. When all meatballs are browned, pour undiluted consommé into skillet. Bring to a boil, stirring vigorously to scrape up bits of meat from skillet. Stirring constantly, boil until mixture is reduced to a thick, syrupy glaze, 10 to 15 minutes. Arrange hot cooked meatballs in a shallow serving dish. Pour glaze over meatballs. Serve hot. Makes 6 main-dish servings, or about 50 tiny meatballs.

Apple-Stuffed Pork Loin

Fylt Svinekam—Norway

Fruit holds moisture and makes this roast tender and juicy.

1 boneless pork loin roast (4 to 6 pounds)
1 green apple, peeled, cored, sliced
10 pitted prunes
1 tablespoon salt
1 teaspoon freshly ground black pepper
3 cups chicken or beef broth, beer, or water

Preheat oven to 350°F (175°C). Lay meat on a flat surface, fat-side down. Arrange apple slices and prunes over surface of roast. Sprinkle with 1 teaspoon salt and ½ teaspoon pepper. Tightly roll up roast, enclosing filling. Tie in at least 3 places with kitchen twine. Rub outside of roast with remaining salt and pepper. Place rolled roast in a deep roasting pan. Bake 2½ to 3 hours or until meat is tender when pierced with a fork, or until an instant-reading thermometer inserted into the flesh (not stuffing) registers 155–160°F for medium doneness or 165–170°F for well done. Baste every 30 minutes with about ½ cup broth, beer, or water. Place cooked meat on a hot platter; keep warm. Pour juices from roasting pan through a strainer into a shallow saucepan. Bring to a boil over medium heat. Boil, stirring occasionally, until reduced to about 1 cup of shiny glaze. Remove string from roast and brush roast with glaze. Slice to serve. Makes 8 servings.

Finnish Egg Cheese
Munajuusto—Finland

This mild-flavored, farm-style cheese is excellent with fresh fruits or berries.

4 eggs
3 cups dairy buttermilk
1/2 gallon homogenized whole milk
1½ teaspoons salt
1 teaspoon sugar

In a large bowl, beat eggs with a whisk; beat in buttermilk until blended. In a 4-quart saucepan, bring milk to a boil over medium heat. Stirring constantly, slowly add egg mixture and bring mixture to a boil; immediately remove from heat. Curds will separate from whey in about 1 minute, without stirring. Again place over medium heat until mixture comes to a boil. Stir in salt and sugar, then immediately remove from heat. Cover and let stand at room temperature 30 minutes or until curds rise to top of mixture. Line a colander or strainer over a large bowl. Gently pour curds-and-whey mixture into lined colander or strainer. Let drain 10 minutes. Fold ends of cloth over curds. Gently lift curds in cloth; fit into a cheese mold or any form with drainage holes in bottom, such as a clean flowerpot. Place a weight on top of cloth. Set mold in a dish large enough to catch dippings; refrigerate 24 hours. Discard whey or use to make bread. Remove cheese from mold; unwrap cheese. Serve immediately, or preheat oven to 450°F (230°C). Place cheese on an ungreased baking sheet; brush with melted butter. Bake 10 to 15 minutes or until browned. Makes ½ to ¾ pound cheese.

Danish Rum Pudding

Rombudding—Denmark

Serve this smooth pudding with Raspberry Sauce (page 202) or fill the center with fresh berries.

2 envelopes unflavored gelatin (¼ ounce each)
¼ cup cold water
5 egg yolks
¾ cup sugar
2 cups hot milk
¼ cup light rum
1 cup whipping cream, whipped
Fresh raspberries or Raspberry Sauce, if desired

Lightly oil a 1½-quart fancy dessert mold; set aside. In a small bowl, sprinkle gelatin over water; set aside to soften, 2 to 3 minutes. In top of double boiler or in a large metal bowl, beat egg yolks until frothy. Slowly beat in sugar and milk until light and lemon colored. Place over simmering water. Stirring constantly, cook 10 minutes or until smooth and creamy. Stir in rum, then gelatin mixture. Cover and refrigerate until mixture begins to set, about 45 minutes. Fold in whipped cream. Pour into prepared mold. Refrigerate 4 to 6 hours or until set. Invert onto a serving dish. Serve with raspberries or Raspberry Sauce, if desired. Makes 6 to 8 servings.

Variation
Substitute 1 teaspoon rum extract for rum. Use only 1 envelope (¼ ounce) unflavored gelatin.

Raspberry Sauce
Hindbærsauce—Denmark

Serve this sauce over rum pudding, cake, or ice cream.

   1 package frozen raspberries (10 ounces), thawed
   ¾ cup red currant jelly
   1 tablespoon cornstarch

In a medium saucepan, combine raspberries with juice, jelly, and cornstarch.
Bring to a boil over medium heat, stirring constantly. Cook and stir until
thickened. Cool. Makes 2 cups.

Hot Wine Punch

Glögg—Sweden

This spicy wine punch is a wintertime favorite in Scandinavia.

1 medium orange
2 liters dry red wine
2 liters dry white wine
2 cups light or dark raisins
12 whole cardamom pods, white part removed, seeds bruised
10 whole cloves
1 piece of gingerroot (2 inches), peeled
1 cinnamon stick (3 inches)
¼ to ½ cup sugar
2 cups whole blanched almonds

Use a vegetable peeler to cut colored peel, or zest, from orange. Be careful not to get any white pith. Use orange for another purpose. In a 6- to 8-quart non-aluminum pot, combine orange peel, wines, raisins, cardamom, cloves, gingerroot, and cinnamon stick. Cover and let stand 12 to 24 hours to let flavors blend. Shortly before serving, bring to a simmer over medium heat. Do not boil. Stir in sugar to taste until dissolved. Stir in almonds. Serve hot punch in mugs. Makes 12 to 15 servings.

Variations

For a nonalcoholic punch, substitute white grape juice or apple cider for wine.

Flaming Glögg

Omit sugar. As wine mixture heats, place about 20 sugar cubes and 1½ cups aquavit, schnapps, rum, brandy, or cognac into a small saucepan. Stir over low heat until warmed. Use a long-stemmed match to ignite alcohol and sugar mixture. Holding a strainer over the wine mixture, pour the flaming alcohol and sugar mixture through the strainer and into the wine. When flame goes out, stir any sugar remaining in the strainer into the punch. Stir in almonds before serving.

Parent's Day Smörgåsbord

MENU

FIRST COURSE:

Herring Fillets

COLD FOOD COURSE:

Salted Salmon, Veal Terrine (page xviii)

Mushroom Salad, West Coast Salad

HOT FOOD COURSE:

Spicy Marinated Pork

Boneless Birds

Gingered Brown Beans

Carrot Casserole

Rutabaga-Potato Casserole

Danish Pumpernickel (page 247)

Potato Flatbread (page 45)

Emmentaler, Gjetost, Danablu, Edam Cheeses

Baked Bread Cheese

DESSERT COURSE:

Finnish Air Pudding

Veiled Country Lass

Blueberry Bars (page 282)

Red or White Wine, Coffee, Tea

FATHER'S DAY WAS FIRST CELEBRATED in Scandinavia in 1931. On the second Sunday in November, father is usually awakened in the morning with a breakfast tray. It contains his favorite pastry, morning cup of coffee, flowers, and a gift. The day centers around father, with everyone thinking of things to make his day special. Dinner includes father's favorite foods, and he invites his favorite friends. Food choices may include a variety of meats and potatoes, but herring, cheese, and bread are always on the menu.

Most Scandinavian fathers enjoy salted fish. Salted fish has remained a favorite of Scandinavians from the days when they preserved fish and other meats by salting them. The salting process breaks down the muscle tissues, giving you a tender texture and a mild flavor. Salted Salmon is a smörgåsbord favorite. It is used on open-face sandwiches and as an appetizer. It is expensive when bought in a store, but much less so when prepared at home by the easy method in my recipe.

Mother's Day is celebrated the last Sunday in May and is an equally good excuse for a special meal. Be sure to plan it so mother can escape the work. Mother's Day became an annual holiday in Sweden in 1919 and is now celebrated in all of Scandinavia. It was borrowed from England, where it had existed as *Mothering Sunday* since the seventeenth century.

But in 1919, there were problems. Mother was probably the only family member who knew how to plan and carry out a celebration or tradition. Therefore, it was necessary to publish a set of instructions for other family members.

The following *Mors Dag* instructions were published in Sweden in 1920:

1. Raise the Flag.
2. Greet Mother with songs in the morning.
3. Serve coffee and coffeecake before she gets out of bed.
4. Give her flowers and a small gift.

In the afternoon, the family takes a torte or cake and a bouquet of spring flowers—primroses or anemones—to Grandmother. The cake is usually fancy, rich, and cream filled, such as Strawberry Cream Cake (page 157).

If this is a tradition you want to start in your family, take Grandmother her favorite cake. A young friend of ours has adopted a "grandmother" in a nearby nursing home. She often enjoys gifts such as this.

Long spring days bring all of Scandinavia to an intense and fruitful summer season. The sun doesn't quite set as it skims the horizon at midnight. It force-feeds the countryside into greenness and gardens into a pageant of flowers. Vegetables and fruits mature early.

In appreciation of springtime after a long winter, Scandinavians place leafy branches from silver birch trees on either side of entrances to buildings, restaurants, apartment buildings, shops, and homes. Everywhere you look, doors, decks, gardens, patios—even balconies on high-rise apartment buildings—are decorated with leaves and flowers.

Select and prepare two or more dishes from each course in this Parent's Day Smörgåsbord.

Herring Fillets

Sildfiller med Saser—Scandinavia

This herring is delectable with or without the sauces.

    1 pound salted or brined herring
    Horseradish Sauce (see below)
    Curry-Mayonnaise Sauce (see below)
    ¼ chopped fresh chives
    ¼ cup chopped green onion with tops
    1 cup dairy sour cream

Horseradish Sauce
    ½ cup whipping cream
    ¼ teaspoon lemon juice
    ⅛ teaspoon sugar
    2 tablespoons grated fresh horseradish

Curry-Mayonnaise Sauce
    ½ cup mayonnaise
    ¼ cup whipping cream, whipped
    ½ teaspoon curry powder
    ¼ teaspoon paprika
    ½ teaspoon dried dill weed, crumbled
    ½ teaspoon dried leaf oregano, crumbled

In refrigerator, soak herring overnight in cold water to cover. Prepare Horseradish Sauce and Curry-Mayonnaise Sauce 1 or 2 hours before serving. Drain fish; remove head, tail, skin, and backbone. Rinse in cold water. Cut fish crosswise into ¾-inch slices. Arrange herring slices on a serving tray or board. Place chopped chives, chopped green onion, and sour cream in separate small bowls. Let guests spoon a sauce or sour cream over top. Garnish with chives or green onion. Makes 16 to 20 herring pieces.

Horseradish Sauce

In a small bowl, whip cream until soft peaks form. Stir in remaining ingredients. Makes ¾ cup.

Curry-Mayonnaise Sauce

In a small bowl, blend all ingredients. Makes 1 cup.

Salted Salmon

Gravlax—Scandinavian

This simple-to-prepare dish is popular in all Scandinavian countries.

2 pounds fresh salmon fillet
½ cup chopped fresh dill or 2 tablespoons dried dill weed, crumbled
¼ cup salt
¼ cup sugar
¼ teaspoon ground white pepper
¼ teaspoon ground allspice

Rinse salmon; dry with paper towels. Place in a 13 x 9-inch glass dish. Sprinkle with half of dill. In a small bowl, combine salt, sugar, white pepper, and allspice. Sprinkle half of mixture over fish; turn fish over and sprinkle with remaining salt mixture. Top with remaining dill. Cover with plastic wrap; refrigerate 24 hours. If a compact texture is desired, place a 12 x 7-inch dish on top of fish. Place several cans of food in top dish for weight. Occasionally spoon juices over fish. To serve, drain fish and cut diagonally in ⅛-inch slices. Arrange on a platter. Makes 12 appetizer servings.

Mushroom Salad
Sienisalaatti—Finland

Finns make this salad with wild mushrooms when they are in season.

1 pound mushrooms, thinly sliced
2 tablespoons grated onion
2 tablespoons lemon juice
2 teaspoons sugar
½ teaspoon freshly ground black pepper
½ cup whipping cream
¼ cup dairy sour cream
1 teaspoon salt
⅛ teaspoon ground white pepper
⅛ teaspoon ground allspice
Crisp lettuce leaves
1 tomato, cut in wedges
Fresh dill or parsley sprigs for garnish

In a large bowl, combine mushrooms, onion, lemon juice, sugar, and black pepper. In a small bowl, beat whipping cream until soft peaks form. Fold in sour cream, salt, white pepper, and allspice. Fold cream mixture into mushroom mixture. Line salad platter or bowl with lettuce leaves. Add mushroom mixture; garnish with tomato wedges and dill or parsley sprigs. Makes 8 servings.

West Coast Salad

Västkustsallat—Sweden

A must for the smörgåsbord table; also serve this beautiful salad for lunch or supper.

Garlic Dressing (see below)
Crisp lettuce leaves
1 pound fresh asparagus, cut in 1-inch pieces, cooked
½ pound mushrooms, sliced
1 can beets (16 ounces), cut in julienne pieces
1 cup frozen baby peas, thawed
3 tomatoes, cut in wedges
3 hard-cooked eggs, quartered
1 cup cooked tiny shrimp
2 packages frozen crabmeat (6 ounces each), thawed, drained
3 tablespoons minced fresh parsley

Garlic Dressing

2 garlic cloves, minced or mashed
2 teaspoons Dijon mustard
2 tablespoons white wine vinegar
¼ cup olive or vegetable oil
3 tablespoons minced fresh dill

Prepare Garlic Dressing; set aside. Line a large shallow bowl or platter with lettuce leaves. Over lettuce, arrange asparagus, mushrooms, beets, peas, tomatoes, eggs, shrimp, and crabmeat. Sprinkle with parsley. Serve immediately with Garlic Dressing. Makes 8 luncheon servings.

Garlic Dressing

In a medium bowl, combine garlic, mustard, and vinegar. Use a whisk to beat in oil until dressing is thick. Fold in dill.

Spicy Marinated Pork

Stegt Svinekam—Denmark

In Scandinavia, fresh juniper berries are picked from cedar trees.

1 boneless pork loin roast (4 to 6 pounds), rolled, tied
1½ cups red port wine
½ cup red wine vinegar
1 tablespoon juniper berries or whole allspice
1 tablespoon ground allspice
1 tablespoon ground ginger
1 teaspoon salt
½ cup whipping cream
2 tablespoons crumbled blue cheese (½ ounce)
2 tablespoons red currant or wild plum jelly

Wipe meat with paper towels to remove moisture; set aside. In a large, deep nonmetal bowl, combine wine, vinegar, juniper berries or whole allspice, ground allspice, ginger, and salt. Add meat, turning several times to coat evenly. Cover and refrigerate at least 6 hours or overnight, turning once or twice. To bake, 3½ to 4 hours before serving, preheat oven to 325°F (165°C). Remove meat from marinade. Insert a meat thermometer into center of roast. Place on a rack in a medium roasting pan. Pour marinade into bottom of pan. Bake until thermometer registers 155–160°F for medium doneness or 165–170°F for well done, about 3 hours. Baste 3 or 4 times during roasting. Place meat on a hot platter; keep warm. To make a sauce, skim fat from pan drippings. Pour drippings through a strainer into a medium saucepan. Bring drippings to a boil over high heat; stir in cream. Reduce heat until mixture boils gently. Stirring occasionally, boil until liquid is reduced to 1½ cups. Stir in blue cheese and jelly. Beat gently with a whisk until dissolved. Pour sauce into a medium serving bowl. To serve, slice roast; spoon sauce over individual servings. Makes 8 servings.

Boneless Birds

Okserulader—Norway

Stuffed-and-rolled meat is a favorite in all of the Scandinavian countries.

2 pounds beef round steak, sliced ¼ inch thick
1 teaspoon salt
½ teaspoon ground allspice
¼ pound mushrooms, chopped
¼ pound bacon, diced
2 tablespoons chopped parsley
1 small onion, sliced lengthwise
2 tablespoons all-purpose flour
2 tablespoons butter
½ cup beef broth
½ cup half-and-half

Cut meat into 8 equal pieces. Place between pieces of plastic wrap. With flat side of a meat mallet, pound until meat is thin and almost doubled in size. Sprinkle flattened meat with salt and allspice. Evenly spoon mushrooms, bacon, parsley, and onion on top of seasoned meat pieces. Roll up tightly, jelly-roll fashion, and secure with wooden picks or tie with cotton string. Roll meat rolls in flour. Melt butter in a large, heavy skillet over medium heat. Add meat rolls; brown on all sides. As rolls are browned, place in an oven-to-table casserole dish. Preheat oven to 300°F (150°C). Add broth and half-and-half to drippings in skillet; stir over medium-low heat until thickened. Pour over meat rolls. Cover and bake 1 hour or until meat is tender. Makes 8 servings.

Gingered Brown Beans

Bruna Böner—Sweden

This traditional Swedish brown-bean dish has a pleasant sweet-sour flavor.

2 cups Swedish brown beans or pinto beans
5 cups water
1 teaspoon salt
2 teaspoons chopped crystallized ginger
¼ cup cider vinegar
¼ cup dark corn syrup
¼ cup packed brown sugar
1 teaspoon ground ginger
Salt, vinegar, and corn syrup, if desired

Rinse and pick over beans. Place in a large saucepan with water and 1 teaspoon salt. Let stand overnight. Retaining water that beans were soaked in, bring to a boil over medium-high heat. Add crystallized ginger. Cover and simmer over low heat 1½ hours or until beans are tender. Use a potato masher to crush some of the beans. Stir in ¼ cup vinegar, ¼ cup syrup, brown sugar, and ground ginger. Simmer 30 minutes longer or until thickened. Taste and add more salt, vinegar, and syrup, if desired. Makes 6 to 8 servings.

Carrot Casserole

Porkkanalaatikko—Finland

This is nutritious enough to be a main dish for a meatless meal.

1 cup cooked rice
2 cups milk
4 cups shredded peeled carrots
1 teaspoon salt
1 tablespoon brown sugar
2 eggs, slightly beaten
3 tablespoons butter
⅓ cup fine dry breadcrumbs

Butter a 2-quart casserole dish; set aside. Preheat oven to 375°F (190°C). In a large bowl, combine rice, milk, carrots, salt, brown sugar, and eggs. Pour into prepared casserole dish. Melt butter in a small skillet; stir in bread-crumbs. Sprinkle buttered crumbs over top of casserole. Bake 45 minutes or until set and carrots are tender. Makes 4 to 8 servings.

To Cook Rice

In a medium saucepan, combine 1 cup rice, 2 cups water, and 1 teaspoon salt. Bring to a rolling boil, then lower heat until the water just simmers. Cover and simmer 15 to 20 minutes until the water is absorbed. To pre-pare in the microwave, combine rice, water, and salt in a deep, 2-quart glass dish. Cover and microwave at full power, 5 minutes or until mixture boils. Microwave at medium, or 50% power, 15 to 20 minutes until water is absorbed.

Rutabaga-Potato Casserole
Perunalanttulaatikko—Finland

This casserole can be assembled a day in advance and baked just before serving.

> 2 pounds rutabagas or turnips, peeled, diced
> ½ pound potatoes, peeled, diced
> 4 cups water
> ⅓ cup all-purpose flour
> ½ cup soft breadcrumbs
> ⅓ cup whipping cream
> ⅓ dark corn syrup
> ¼ cup butter, melted
> 2 eggs, beaten
> 1 teaspoon salt
> ½ teaspoon ground allspice
> ½ teaspoon ground nutmeg
> ½ teaspoon ground ginger
> ¼ teaspoon ground white pepper
> 2 to 3 tablespoons butter, melted

In a large saucepan, combine rutabagas or turnips and potatoes; add water. Bring to a boil; cook over low heat 25 minutes or until tender. Drain, reserving cooking liquid. Mash rutabagas or turnips and potatoes until smooth. Butter a shallow 2-quart casserole dish; set aside. Preheat oven to 300°F (150°C). In large bowl of electric mixer, beat potato mixture on high speed, adding ½ cup cooking liquid during beating. Beat in flour, breadcrumbs, cream, syrup, ¼ cup melted butter, eggs, salt, allspice, nutmeg, ginger, and white pepper. Beat until light and fluffy. Spoon into prepared casserole dish. Use a spoon to smooth top. Drizzle with 2 to 3 tablespoons melted butter. Bake, uncovered, 1½ to 2 hours or until surface is lightly browned. Makes 8 servings.

Baked Bread Cheese

Leipäjuusto—Finland

Look for rennet tablets at your pharmacy; they can be ordered if not regularly in stock. Also, using unhomogenized milk (it can be pasteurized) will increase your chances for success in making this cheese. Have on hand a rimmed pizza pan for baking the cheese.

½ rennet tablet
¼ cup cool chlorine-free water
2 gallons milk (whole, 2%, 1%, or skim), preferably unhomogenized
2 teaspoons citric acid or lemon juice
1 teaspoon coarse kosher salt
2 teaspoons sugar

Crush the rennet tablet into the water and stir to dissolve. Pour milk into a non-aluminum or non-cast-iron pot. Place over medium heat. Sprinkle the citric acid over the milk and stir 2–3 times. Heat milk to 88°F (check with a cheese or candy thermometer). Milk will begin to curdle.

At 88°F, add the rennet solution and continue stirring slowly every few minutes until the milk reaches 105°F. Turn off the heat and stop stirring. Cover and let stand for 30 minutes. The milk will separate into a solid curd, with whey (the clear, greenish liquid) around the edges. The curd will split in a straight line when cut with a knife. With a long knife, cut the curd into 1-inch cubes. Cover and let stand 1 hour longer.

Line a large colander or strainer with a damp towel or several layers of damp cheesecloth; place over a large bowl. Pour curds and whey into the lined colander. Pour off whey and let drain 1 hour longer or until whey no longer drips from the bottom of the colander. Butter a 12- to 14-inch pizza pan with raised sides. Pat drained curds into pizza pan. Place pan on a baking sheet with raised sides. Elevate one side of the pizza pan to let whey drain into baking sheet. Preheat broiler. Sprinkle top of cheese with ½ teaspoon kosher salt and 1 teaspoon sugar. Broil 8 inches from heat until browned in spots, 25 to 30 minutes; pour excess whey from baking sheet; wipe baking sheet with a damp cloth. Invert cheese onto a cleaned baking sheet. Sprinkle with remaining salt and sugar. Return to broiler; broil until browned in spots and cheese is about ½ inch thick. Cool; cut in wedges. Makes one 12- to 14-inch bread cheese. Serving suggestion: serve with cloudberry jam or with berries.

Finnish Air Pudding

Ilmapuuro—Finland

This old-time Finnish favorite is simple and spectacular.

3 cups cranberry juice
6 tablespoons sugar
Pinch salt
½ cup uncooked farina or Cream of Wheat
About 1 cup half-and-half

In large saucepan, combine cranberry juice, sugar, salt, and farina or Cream of Wheat. Stirring constantly, bring to a boil over medium heat. Cook and stir 8 minutes or until thickened. Pour into large bowl of electric mixer. Beat 15 minutes at highest speed. Pudding will become pale pink and volume will increase to about 4 times the original. Pour into a serving bowl; serve immediately or refrigerate until ready to serve. Spoon about 2 tablespoons of half-and-half over each serving. Makes 8 servings.

Veiled Country Lass

Bondepige med Slør—Denmark

Layers of rye breadcrumbs, applesauce, raspberry jam, chocolate, and whipped cream—yum!

2 tablespoons butter
1 cup dry rye breadcrumbs or dry chocolate-cake crumbs
2 tablespoons sugar
½ cup raspberry jam
3 cups chunk-style applesauce
½ cup grated sweet chocolate
1 cup whipping cream, softly whipped

Melt butter in a small skillet over medium heat. Stir in breadcrumbs or cake crumbs and sugar until crumbs are crisp and completely buttered. Spoon one-third of crumb mixture into bottom of a glass serving bowl. Add one-third of the raspberry jam in small dollops. Over jam, spread a layer of about one-third each of the applesauce, chocolate, and whipped cream. Repeat layering, saving a little chocolate to sprinkle over top layer of whipped cream to make a fine *veil*. Refrigerate until ready to serve. Makes 6 to 8 servings.

Low-Calorie Whipped Topping
Combine ½ cup nonfat dry milk and ⅓ cup ice water in a deep, medium bowl. Beat with an electric mixer until mixture is thick and stands in soft peaks. Add 1 tablespoon lemon juice. Continue beating until stiff peaks form. Sweeten to taste.

Specialty Baking

TWICE-BAKED BREADS, RUSKS, AND TOASTS are found in abundance throughout Scandinavia. You see them in glass jars or bins in bread shops where they can be purchased by the kilo. It is a sensible way to store bread, especially in the summertime when it may be too warm to use the oven. Rusk-making was a Saturday activity in country homes. Breads left from the previous week's baking were sliced and dried in the oven, making pale, dry toast that kept well in an airtight container. Breadmaking usually occurred on Saturday and there would be fresh bread and fresh toast for the following week. Toast made from sweet yeast bread is often dunked in coffee. Rusks are eaten for breakfast, snacks, and lunch.

Hardtack, crisp bread, and flatbread were also kept in airtight containers during the summer. One Norwegian grandmother told me she made her flour lefse, wrapped it in waxed paper, and kept it in a box under her bed. Hardtack and crisp breads resemble crackers. They are excellent eaten with a spread of butter or a simple topping of cheese or cold cuts. Flour lefse is not usually served crisp, but is dipped in hot water, then placed between cloths or towels until soft and pliable. Then it is buttered, sprinkled with sugar or cinnamon-sugar, rolled or folded, and cut into bite-size pieces. Potato lefse does not become crisp when cooked, but resembles a thin Mexican flour tortilla. Potato lefse can be prepared several weeks ahead, wrapped airtight, and stored in the freezer. Unwrap it to thaw.

Lingonberry Spice Cake

Pepperkake—Norway

Lingonberries or cranberries give this pound cake a gentle tartness.

¾ cup butter, room temperature
1¼ cups granulated sugar
4 eggs
2 teaspoons ground cinnamon
1 teaspoon ground ginger
1 teaspoon ground cloves
2 teaspoons baking powder
1 teaspoon baking soda
1 teaspoon salt
3 cups all-purpose flour
1½ cups dairy sour cream
2 to 4 tablespoons fresh or canned whole lingonberries, drained, or
    chopped fresh cranberries
2 to 3 tablespoons powdered sugar

Preheat oven to 350°F (175°C). Butter a 10-cup Bundt® pan. Dust pan lightly with flour. In large bowl of electric mixer, cream butter and granulated sugar until smooth. Beat in eggs until light and fluffy. In a medium bowl, stir together cinnamon, ginger, cloves, baking powder, baking soda, salt, and flour. Alternately stir flour mixture and sour cream into sugar mixture until smooth. Fold in lingonberries or cranberries. Pour into prepared pan. Bake about 55 minutes or until a skewer inserted into cake comes out clean. Invert onto a rack; remove pan. Cool, then dust with powdered sugar. Place on serving plate. Makes about 12 servings.

Almond-Caramel Cake

Toskakake—Norway

Crunchy, almond topping coats this rich cake.

1 cup whipping cream
2 eggs
1 teaspoon vanilla extract
1½ cups all-purpose flour
1 cup sugar
2 teaspoons baking powder
½ teaspoon salt
Caramel Topping (see below)

Caramel Topping

⅓ cup butter
⅓ cup sugar
¾ cup chopped almonds
1 tablespoon all-purpose flour
1 tablespoon whipping cream

Preheat oven to 350°F (175°C). Butter a 10-inch springform pan or tart pan with a removable bottom; set aside. In large bowl of electric mixer, beat cream until stiff; beat in eggs and vanilla. In a small bowl, stir together flour, sugar, baking powder, and salt. Beat flour mixture into cream mixture until smooth. Pour into prepared pan. Bake 40 minutes or until cake pulls away from side of pan. Prepare Caramel Topping. Pour hot topping over hot cake, completely covering top. Bake 15 to 20 minutes longer or until golden brown. Remove sides from springform pan. Serve warm or cold. Makes 8 to 10 servings.

Caramel Topping

Melt butter in a small saucepan over medium heat. Add remaining ingredients. Stirring constantly, bring to a boil. Continue stirring until slightly thickened, 3 to 5 minutes.

Danish Pancake Balls

Æbleskiver—Denmark

These pancake balls are sometimes called "munk," and are eaten as doughnuts.

½ cup butter, melted
3 eggs, separated
1 cup milk
2 tablespoons sugar
1½ cups all-purpose flour
2 teaspoons baking powder
½ teaspoon salt
½ teaspoon ground cardamom, if desired
Powdered sugar
Butter for pan

In a large bowl, blend ½ cup melted butter, egg yolks, milk, and sugar. In a medium bowl, combine flour, baking powder, salt, and cardamom, if desired. Stir into egg-yolk mixture. In a clean medium bowl, beat egg whites until stiff but not dry. Fold into flour mixture. Heat *æbleskiver pan* (page xv) over medium-low heat until a drop of water sizzles when dropped into pan. Spoon ½ teaspoon butter into each cup; let melt. Spoon 1 rounded tablespoon batter into each cup. Cook about 1 minute on each side, using a knitting needle or long wooden skewer to turn balls. If heat is too high, centers will be doughy. Dust each with powdered sugar. Serve hot. Makes 20 pancake balls.

Variation
Filled Æbleskiver: Spoon 1 teaspoon applesauce onto center of uncooked batter in each cup. Top with about ½ teaspoon additional batter to enclose applesauce. Cook as directed above.

Cream Twists

Kringler—Norway

Not a cookie, bread, or cake, but a favorite pastry, buttered and served warm with coffee.

1 cup sugar
1 egg
1 cup whipping cream
1 cup dairy sour cream
1 teaspoon salt
2 teaspoons baking powder
1 teaspoon vanilla extract
3½ cups all-purpose flour

In a large bowl, combine sugar, egg, and whipping cream; beat until light and fluffy. Add sour cream, salt, baking powder, and vanilla and beat again until light and fluffy. Slowly stir in flour, making a stiff dough. Turn out onto a lightly floured board. Knead only long enough to make a smooth ball. Wrap in plastic wrap; refrigerate overnight. Preheat oven to 450°F (230°C). Lightly grease a large baking sheet; set aside. Turn out dough onto a lightly floured board. Cut into fourths. Refrigerate 3 portions. Cut remaining portion into 12 equal pieces. Roll each piece between your hands to make an 8-inch rope. Shape each into a figure 8. Pinch ends to seal. Arrange shaped dough, 2 inches apart, on prepared baking sheet. Bake 6 to 8 minutes or until lightly browned. Cool slightly. Repeat with remaining dough. Place warm rolls in a container with a tight cover to keep them soft and puffy. Wipe moisture from inside of lid as it gathers, so rolls do not become wet. Freeze, if desired. Serve warm. Makes 48 rolls.

Mrs. Olson's Flour Lefse

Nordlenning Krinelefse—Norway

Dry flour lefse is dipped in water to soften before it is served.

2 cups milk
¼ cup vegetable shortening or lard
1 teaspoon salt
2 cups all-purpose flour
Egg Glaze (page 241)
Soft butter
Sugar, if desired
Cinnamon, if desired

In a medium saucepan, bring milk to a boil with shortening or lard and salt. Add flour all at once and stir until very thick. Mixture will resemble cream-puff paste. Remove from heat and cool. Mixture should be very thick but pliable. Divide into fourths. Divide each into 4 equal parts, making 16 pieces. Shape each into a ball, then flatten slightly. Preheat a griddle to 375°F (190°C). On a lightly floured board, roll 1 ball of dough at a time into a paper-thin 10- or 11-inch circle. Use a grooved *lefse rolling pin* (page xvi) to get authentic grid-like texture. Bake dough circles on ungreased preheated griddle, 1 to 2 minutes on each side until browned in spots. Lefse will look dry, but will be flexible, not dry and crisp. Stack baked lefse on a square of waxed paper. Prepare Egg Glaze. When all lefse are baked, brush them, 1 at a time, with glaze. Again place each on griddle, glazed-side up; bake until glaze is dry. Again stack on waxed paper, glazed-side down. *To serve immediately,* brush with soft butter; sprinkle with sugar and cinnamon, if desired. Roll up and cut diagonally into 2-inch slices. Arrange on a bread tray. *To serve later,* store in a cool dry place, loosely wrapped in waxed paper. Lefse will become dry and crisp. Before serving, dip quickly into hot water and stack between cloths or sheets of plastic wrap until soft. Brush with soft butter; sprinkle with sugar and cinnamon, if desired. Roll and cut as directed above, or fold in half and cut into wedges or 2-inch slices. Makes 16 lefse.

Oatmeal Hardtack

Knäckebröd—Sweden

Serve these tender, crisp crackers with cheese and soup.

½ cup vegetable shortening
¼ cup butter, room temperature
½ cup sugar
2 cups uncooked rolled oats (regular or quick-cooking)
3 cups all-purpose flour
1½ teaspoons salt
1 teaspoon baking soda
1½ cups buttermilk

In a large bowl, cream shortening, butter, and sugar until smooth. In a medium bowl, combine oats, flour, salt, and baking soda. Alternately add flour mixture and buttermilk to creamed mixture, blending until stiff like a cookie dough. Refrigerate 30 minutes. Grease a large baking sheet; sprinkle with rolled oats. Preheat oven to 325°F (165°C). Divide dough into 8 equal portions. Shape each portion into a smooth ball. Return 7 balls of dough to bowl; cover and refrigerate. Place remaining ball of dough on prepared baking sheet. Flatten as much as possible with your hands, then use a rolling pin to roll dough to edges of baking sheet. Using a *hardtack rolling pin* (page xv) make pebbled imprints on top, or prick evenly with tines of a fork to make a rough texture. Use a pastry wheel, knife, or pizza cutter to score dough in 2-inch squares. Bake 15 to 20 minutes or until crisp and golden. Cool 3 minutes on baking sheet, then place on a rack to finish cooling. Break into crackers where scored. Repeat with remaining dough. Makes about 128 crackers.

Loaves of bread or individual rolls can be freshened by quickly dipping them in and out of cold water, then baking them in a preheated 350°F (175°C) oven for 10 minutes.

Scandinavian Yeast Breads

VISITORS TO SCANDINAVIA ARE OVERWHELMED with the breads. There are dark rye breads, whole-wheat breads, white breads, and multiple-grain breads. There are fat loaves, thin loaves, round loaves, crisp breads, flatbreads, buns, rusks, and sweet breads. They are the heaviest and the most delicious breads I have ever eaten!

Rye, barley, and oats are the grains native to the area. They are quick growing and mature early in the intensity of long, sunny, summer days. For centuries these grains have been used in the breads of Scandinavia. Some wheat is grown in Sweden and Denmark, but most is imported.

There is a difference between the *rye meal* and *rye flour* called for in the following recipes. Rye meal is also called *pumpernickel rye, dark rye,* or *coarse rye*. Rye meal contains bran. Rye flour is usually labeled *light rye* or *medium rye*. When making breads that call for rye flour, either light or medium is suitable. It is possible to interchange rye flour and rye meal, but the texture will be different.

Soured-rye loaves have played an important part in bread baking. Years ago, salt was an expensive imported seasoning and sourdough starter was the only yeast available. Because of its tangy flavor, sourdough bread needs very little salt. Thus, soured-rye bread was the answer. Part of the dough was saved each time as a starter for the next batch of bread, or dough was mixed in a large wooden bowl that was not washed between bakings. The sourdough starter was saved in dry, crusty pieces of dough left in the bowl.

The custom of baking breads and cookies in animal shapes, especially at Christmastime, goes back to pagan days. It was a ritual to burn offerings to the gods. Scandinavian farmers were too poor to offer their livestock. Instead, their burnt offerings were goats made of straw and breads and small cakes shaped as animals. Straw goats, called *julbock,* are a popular Christmas ornament today. You can buy some very tiny ones, or those that stand over eighteen inches tall.

Scandinavians excel at baking. They use lots of butter, eggs, and milk, so their baked goods are some of the best in the world. Today, homemakers are not tied to their ovens. There is a wide variety of excellent breads in bakeries, supermarkets, and in the colorful open-market squares that exist in most towns throughout Scandinavia. Here, you will meet Scandinavians who begin their days early, baking the goods they will later sell to the public. Sometimes the breads and pastries are still warm.

St. Lucia Saffron Bread

Saffransbröd—Sweden

*On December 13, a girl is named "Lucia" at home or school and she serves
this bread.*

1 envelope active dry yeast (¼ ounce)
¼ cup warm water (110°F, 45°C)
¾ cup milk
1 teaspoon saffron threads or ¹⁄₁₆ teaspoon powdered saffron
½ cup butter
½ cup sugar
1 teaspoon salt
½ cup golden raisins
2 eggs, slightly beaten
3½ to 4 cups all-purpose or bread flour
Egg Glaze (page 241)
¼ cup sliced almonds
¼ cup pearl sugar (page XVII) or coarsely crushed sugar cubes
About ½ cup raisins for St. Lucia Cats

In a small bowl, stir yeast into warm water; let stand 5 minutes to soften. In a
small saucepan, combine milk and saffron. Bring to a boil over medium heat,
stirring until milk turns a deep yellow. Pour through a strainer into a large
bowl. Stir in butter, sugar, salt, and golden raisins. Cool slightly; stir in yeast
mixture and eggs. Beating to keep mixture smooth, stir in enough flour to
make a stiff dough. Turn out onto a lightly floured board. Cover with a dry
cloth; let stand 5 to 15 minutes. Wash and grease bowl; set aside. Grease a
large baking sheet; set aside. Adding flour as needed to prevent sticking, knead
dough until smooth, about 10 minutes. Place in greased bowl, turning to
grease all sides. Cover and let rise in a warm place until doubled in bulk, about
2 hours. Punch down dough; turn out onto a lightly oiled surface. Shape into a
Candle Wreath or St. Lucia Cats (see below). Place shaped dough on prepared
baking sheet; let rise in a warm place until doubled in bulk, about 1 hour.

Preheat oven to 375°F (190°C). Brush tops of raised dough with Egg Glaze. Sprinkle with sliced almonds and pearl sugar or crushed sugar cubes. Bake 20 to 25 minutes or until lightly browned; do not overbake. Cool on a rack. Makes 1 St. Lucia Candle Wreath or about 20 St. Lucia Cats.

Shape Variations

St. Lucia Candle Wreath: Divide dough into 3 equal pieces. Roll each piece between palms of your hands and lightly floured surface to make ropes, 30 inches long. Braid ropes together. Cut about 2 inches or ½ cup dough from end of each braid. Place braid on prepared baking sheet, curving into a wreath. Pinch ends together. Shape reserved dough into a rope about 18 inches long. Tie into a bow. Place bow over seam in wreath. Proceed as directed above.

St. Lucia Cats: Divide dough into 5 equal portions. Divide each portion into 4 equal pieces. Roll each piece between palms of your hands to make 6-inch ropes, about ½ inch thick. Shape each into a letter *S*, coiling ends in spirals. Lay 1 shaped rope across another, with center of top rope touching center of bottom rope. All spirals will curve in same direction. Press 1 raisin into center of each spiral. Let rise until doubled. Brush with Egg Glaze. Sprinkle with pearl sugar. Bake as directed above.

Saffron gives some Scandinavian yeast breads a special flavor and yellow color, but it is expensive. To give a yellow color, substitute ground turmeric for the saffron. Add nutmeg or cardamom for a different but pleasant flavor.

Shrove Tuesday Buns

Semlor—Sweden

These stuffed buns are usually served in a bowl of hot milk, but I prefer Hot Vanilla Sauce (page 235).

1 envelope active dry yeast (¼ ounce)
¼ cup warm water (110°F, 43°C)
1 egg
⅔ cup milk, scalded, cooled
¼ cup granulated sugar
½ teaspoon salt
½ teaspoon ground cardamom or ground cinnamon
½ cup butter, softened
2¾ to 3 cups all-purpose flour
Egg Glaze (page 241)
8 ounces almond paste
½ cup whipping cream, whipped
2 tablespoons powdered sugar
Powdered sugar
Double recipe Hot Vanilla Sauce

In a large bowl, stir yeast into water. Let stand 5 minutes to soften. Beat in egg, milk, granulated sugar, salt, cardamom or cinnamon, and butter. Add 2 cups flour. Beat until smooth and satiny. Add enough of remaining flour to make a stiff dough. Turn out onto a lightly floured board. Cover with a dry cloth; let rest 15 minutes. Clean and lightly oil bowl; set aside. Knead dough 10 minutes or until smooth and satiny. Place in oiled bowl, turning to coat all sides. Cover with dry cloth. Let rise in a warm place until doubled in bulk, about 1 hour. Lightly grease a large baking sheet. Preheat oven to 400°F (205°C). Turn dough out onto a lightly oiled board. Divide dough into fourths. Divide each fourth into 4 parts. Shape each piece of dough into a round bun, about 1 inch high. Place on prepared baking sheet. Let rise until doubled, 45 to 60 minutes. Brush Egg Glaze over top of risen buns.

Baked glazed buns 10 to 12 minutes or until golden brown. Cool on a rack. Cut almond paste into 16 slices. About ⅓ from top, cut horizontally almost through bun, leaving slice attached at 1 side. Insert a slice of almond paste. In a medium bowl, whip cream until soft peaks form; fold in 2 tablespoons powdered sugar. Spoon whipped cream into buns until each is filled and holds top slice open. Or, pipe whipped cream into buns through a pastry bag. Sprinkle powdered sugar over filling and bun. Prepare Hot Vanilla Sauce. To serve, spoon Hot Vanilla Sauce evenly onto 16 dessert dishes; place a filled bun on top of sauce. Unfilled buns may be frozen. To serve, thaw and fill. Makes 16 buns.

It is easier to shape yeast doughs into ropes or balls if you work on a lightly oiled surface rather than on a flour-dusted surface.

Hot Vanilla Sauce

Vaniljesås—Sweden

Use this sauce in place of whipped cream on fruit, pie, or cake, or with Shrove Tuesday Buns.

¼ cup all-purpose flour
⅛ teaspoon salt
¼ cup sugar
4 cups milk
2 teaspoons vanilla extract
1 tablespoon butter

In a medium saucepan, combine flour, salt, and sugar. Slowly stir in milk. Stirring constantly, bring to a boil over medium heat. Cook and stir until thickened. Stir in vanilla and butter until butter melts. Serve hot. Makes 4 cups.

Graham Rusks

Kavring—Norway

In Norway, these twice-baked buns are served for breakfast, or topped with cheese for lunch.

> 1 envelope active dry yeast (¼ ounce)
> 2 cups warm water (110°F, 45°C)
> 3 tablespoons lard or vegetable shortening, melted
> 3 tablespoons sugar
> 1 teaspoon salt
> 2 cups graham flour or whole-wheat flour
> 2 to 2½ cups all-purpose or bread flour

In a large bowl, stir yeast into warm water; let stand 5 minutes to soften. Stir in lard or shortening, sugar, salt, and graham flour or whole-wheat flour. Beat until smooth. Stir in enough all-purpose or bread flour to make a stiff dough. Turn out onto a lightly floured board. Cover with a dry cloth; let stand 5 to 15 minutes. Wash and grease bowl; set aside. Knead dough until smooth, about 10 minutes. Place in greased bowl, turning to grease all sides. Cover and let rise in a warm place until doubled in bulk, about 2 hours. Grease 2 large baking sheets; set aside. Punch down dough; turn out onto a lightly oiled surface. Cut dough in half; divide each half into 12 pieces. Shape each piece into a round ball, 2½ inches in diameter. Arrange buns on prepared baking sheets, about 2 inches apart. Cover and let rise until doubled in bulk, about 45 minutes. Preheat oven to 425°F (220°C). Bake buns 12 to 15 minutes or until golden brown. Cool on racks. When buns are cooled, split horizontally, using 2 forks to pull buns apart. Reduce heat to 250°F (120°C). Place split buns on baking sheets, split-side up; bake until completely dry, about 1 hour. Makes 48 rusks.

Cinnamon Coffee Ring

Kaffekrans—Norway

This no-knead yeast coffeecake is simple, quick, and delicious.

1 envelope active dry yeast (¼ ounce)
1 teaspoon sugar
¼ cup warm water (110°F, 45°C)
1 cup milk, scalded, cooled
¼ cup butter, melted
⅓ cup sugar
1½ teaspoons salt
2½ to 3 cups all-purpose flour
¼ cup butter, room temperature
½ cup sugar
1 tablespoon ground cinnamon
Powdered Sugar Glaze, if desired (see below)

Powdered Sugar Glaze
½ cup powdered sugar
1 to 2 tablespoons hot coffee or water

In a large bowl, stir yeast and 1 teaspoon sugar into warm water; let stand 5 minutes to soften. Stir in milk, ¼ cup melted butter, ⅓ cup sugar, salt, and 1 cup flour. Beat with a spoon or electric mixer until smooth. Gradually stir in 1½ cups flour, keeping dough smooth. If dough is still moist, stir in 1 tablespoon flour at a time to make a soft dough. Cover and let rise in a warm place until doubled in bulk, about 1 hour. Grease a 10- to 12-cup Bundt® pan; set aside. Punch down dough; turn out onto a lightly oiled surface. Roll and stretch dough to make an 18 x 12-inch rectangle. Dough will be soft. Spread with ¼ cup soft butter to within ½ inch of edges. Sprinkle with ½ cup sugar, then with cinnamon. Starting with a 12-inch side, roll up jelly-roll fashion. Place in prepared Bundt® pan, seam-side down. Use scissors to snip halfway through roll, making cuts 1 inch apart. Let rise until dough doubles in bulk and fills pan. Preheat oven to 350°F (175°C). Bake 30 to 40 minutes or until a skewer inserted through center of loaf comes out clean. Cool 5 minutes in pan. Invert onto a rack; remove pan. Cool 15 minutes, then drizzle with glaze. Serve warm or toasted. After mixing in flour, dough can be refrigerated overnight. In morning, shape dough as directed above. Makes 1 coffee ring.

Powdered Sugar Glaze
In a small bowl, combine powdered sugar and coffee or water; beat until smooth.

Shape Variations
Cinnamon Leaves: Divide raised dough in half. On a lightly oiled board, roll and stretch 1 piece of dough to make a 12 x 8-inch rectangle. Spread 2 tablespoons soft butter over top. Sprinkle with ¼ cup sugar and ½ teaspoon ground cinnamon. Beginning on a long side, roll up tightly, jelly-roll fashion. Repeat with remaining dough. Cut rolls into 2-inch slices. Use a sharp knife to make 2 evenly spaced, parallel slashes almost all the way through each 2-inch slice. Place on prepared baking sheets, with slashes up, fanning or pulling apart slightly. Cover and let rise in a warm place until almost doubled in bulk, about 45 minutes. Bake in a 350°F (175°C) oven for 12 to 15 minutes or until golden brown. Top with Powdered Sugar Glaze, if desired. Makes 18 rolls.

Cinnamon Ears: Prepare dough as for Cinnamon Leaves, above, rolling jelly-roll fashion. Cut dough into 2-inch slices. Using the side of your index finger or the handle of a wooden spoon, press on center top of each slice. Edges will turn up. Place on prepared baking sheets. Let rise until doubled in bulk, about 45 minutes. Bake and glaze as for Cinnamon Leaves. Makes 18 rolls.

White Potato Bread

Potetbrød—Norway

This light-textured bread is excellent for sandwiches or toasting.

> 1 envelope active dry yeast (¼ ounce)
> ½ cup warm water or water that potatoes were cooked in (110°F, 45°C)
> ¼ cup sugar
> ½ cup butter, room temperature
> 3 eggs
> 2 teaspoons salt
> 1 cup cooked, mashed potatoes (may be leftover)
> 1 cup milk, scalded, cooled
> 6 to 7 cups all-purpose or bread flour

In a large bowl, stir yeast into warm water or potato water; let stand 5 minutes to soften. Add sugar, butter, eggs, salt, potatoes, and milk; beat until smooth. Adding 1 cup at a time, beat in enough flour to make a stiff dough. Turn out onto a lightly floured board. Cover with a dry cloth; let stand 5 to 15 minutes. Wash and grease bowl; set aside. Grease two 9 x 5-inch loaf pans; set aside. Adding flour as necessary, knead dough until smooth, about 10 minutes. Place in greased bowl, turning to grease all sides. Cover and let rise in a warm place until doubled in bulk, about 2 hours. Punch down dough; divide in half. Shape each half into a loaf. Place in prepared pans; let rise in a warm place until doubled in bulk, 45 to 60 minutes. Preheat oven to 375°F (190°C). Bake 30 to 35 minutes or until loaves are golden brown and sound hollow when tapped with your fingers. Turn out of pans; cool on a rack. Makes 2 loaves.

Holiday Bread

Julekage—Denmark

A favorite in Denmark and Norway.

2 envelopes active dry yeast (¼ ounce each)
¼ cup warm water (110°F, 45°C)
½ cup granulated sugar
2 cups milk, scalded, cooled
2 eggs, slightly beaten
½ cup butter, melted
2 teaspoons salt
1 teaspoon crushed cardamom seeds, if desired
6½ to 7½ cups all-purpose or bread flour
1 cup mixed, diced candied fruits, if desired
1 cup golden raisins
1 cup slivered blanched almonds, if desired
Egg Glaze (below)
¼ cup pearl sugar (page XVII) or coarsely crushed sugar cubes, if desired
Almond Icing (page 257)

In a large bowl, combine yeast, warm water, and 1 tablespoon granulated sugar; let stand 5 minutes to soften. Stir in remaining granulated sugar, milk, eggs, butter, salt, and cardamom, if desired. Add 3 cups flour; beat until smooth. Stir in enough of remaining flour to make a stiff dough. Turn out onto a lightly floured board. Cover with a dry cloth; let stand 8 to 10 minutes. Wash and grease bowl; set aside. Grease 3 round 8- or 9-inch cake pans; set aside. If desired, knead fruits and nuts into dough, adding flour as needed to prevent dough from being sticky. Knead about 10 minutes. Place dough in greased bowl, turning to grease all sides. Cover and let rise in a warm place until doubled in bulk, about 1½ hours. Turn dough out onto a lightly oiled surface; divide dough into thirds. Shape each third into a round loaf; place, seam-side down, in prepared pans. Prepare Egg Glaze. Brush loaves with glaze. Let rise in a warm place until doubled in bulk, about 1 hour. Preheat oven to 375°F (190°C). Again brush loaves with glaze; sprinkle with pearl sugar or crushed sugar cubes, if desired. Bake 25 to 30 minutes or until golden brown and loaves sound hollow when tapped with your fingers. Turn out of pans; cool on a rack. Prepare Almond Icing. Spread over cooled loaves. Makes 3 loaves.

Egg Glaze for Breads and Lefse

In a small bowl, beat together 1 egg, 1 teaspoon salt, and 2 tablespoons milk. Brush glaze over yeast loaves after they have risen and before they are baked. If desired, brush loaves again, 10 minutes before they are taken from the oven. To use with lefse, see Mrs. Olson's Flour Lefse (page 226).

To remove cardamom seeds from pods quickly, place the whole pods in a mortar or between two sheets of waxed paper. Crush the white pods with a pestle or hammer. Lift out the crushed pods and carefully blow onto the seeds to remove any remaining pod pieces. The dark seeds will remain.

Cardamom Coffee Braid

Pulla—Finland

Throughout Scandinavia, this bread is made into a variety of shapes for Christmas.

> 2 envelopes active dry yeast (¼ ounce each)
> ½ cup warm water (110°F, 45°C)
> 2 cups milk, scalded, cooled
> 1 cup granulated sugar
> 2 teaspoons salt
> 1 teaspoon freshly crushed cardamom
> 4 eggs, slightly beaten
> 8 to 9 cups all-purpose or bread flour
> ½ cup butter, melted
> Egg Glaze (page 241)
> ½ cup sliced almonds
> ½ cup pearl sugar (page XVII) or coarsely crushed sugar cubes

In a large bowl, stir yeast into warm water; let stand 5 minutes to soften. Stir in milk, granulated sugar, salt, cardamom, eggs, and 4 cups flour. Beat until smooth. Stir in butter until blended. Gradually stir in enough remaining flour to make a stiff dough. Turn out onto a lightly floured board. Cover with a dry cloth; let stand 5 to 15 minutes. Wash and grease bowl; set aside. Grease 3 large baking sheets; set aside. Adding flour as needed, knead dough until smooth, about 10 minutes. Place dough in bowl, turning to grease all sides. Cover and let rise in a warm place until doubled in bulk, 1½ to 2 hours. Punch down dough; let rise again until doubled in bulk, about 45 minutes. Turn dough out onto a lightly oiled surface. Divide into 3 portions. Working with one-third at a time, divide 1 portion of dough into 3 equal pieces. Roll each piece between palms of your hands and oiled surface to make 3 ropes, 30 inches long. Braid 3 ropes to make a loaf. Pinch ends together and tuck ends under loaf. Repeat with remaining dough. Place 1 braided loaf on each prepared baking sheet. Let rise until doubled in bulk, 45 to 60 minutes.

Preheat oven to 375°F (190°C). Brush loaves with Egg Glaze; sprinkle with sliced almonds and pearl sugar or crushed sugar cubes. Bake 25 to 30 minutes or until crust is lightly browned and tender, not crisp; do not overbake. Cool on racks. Makes 3 braids.

Norwegian Rye Bread

Siktebrød—Norway

Thinly slice and use for Cream Cheese and Salmon Smørrebrød (page 20).

> 1 envelope active dry yeast (¼ ounce)
> ½ warm water (110°F, 45°C)
> 2 cups stirred rye flour
> ¾ cup dark molasses
> ⅓ cup butter
> 1 teaspoon salt
> 2 cups boiling water
> 4½ to 5 cups all-purpose or bread flour

In a small bowl, stir yeast into ½ cup warm water; let stand 5 minutes to soften. In a large bowl of electric mixer, combine rye flour, molasses, butter, and salt. Add boiling water; beat 2 minutes on medium speed. Cool slightly. Stir in yeast mixture. Adding 1 cup at a time, beat in enough all-purpose or bread flour to make a stiff dough. Turn out onto a lightly floured board. Cover with a dry cloth; let stand 5 to 15 minutes. Wash and grease bowl; set aside. Grease two 9 x 5-inch loaf pans; set aside. Adding flour as necessary, knead dough until smooth, about 10 minutes. Place in greased bowl, turning to grease all sides. Cover and let rise in a warm place until doubled in bulk, about 2 hours. Punch down dough; divide in half. Shape each half into a loaf. Place in prepared pans; let rise in a warm place until doubled in bulk, 45 to 60 minutes. Preheat oven to 350°F (175°C). Bake 35 to 45 minutes or until loaves are golden brown and sound hollow when tapped with your fingers. Turn out of pans; cool on a rack. Makes 2 loaves.

Rye Dipping Bread

Doppbröd—Sweden

On Christmas Eve, Swedes dip this bread into the Christmas-ham broth.

1 envelope active dry yeast (¼ ounce)
¼ cup warm water (110°F, 45°C)
1 tablespoon fennel seeds
1 tablespoon anise seeds
1 teaspoon salt
2 tablespoons sugar
2 tablespoons butter, melted
2 cups milk, scalded, cooled
3 cups stirred rye flour
3 to 3½ cups all-purpose or bread flour

In a large bowl, stir yeast into warm water; let stand 5 minutes to soften.
Crush fennel and anise seeds in a mortar and pestle, or pour into a plastic
bag and pound with a hammer. Stir crushed seeds, salt, sugar, butter, milk,
and rye flour into yeast mixture; beat well. Adding 1 cup at a time, beat
in enough all-purpose or bread flour to make a stiff dough. Turn out onto
a lightly floured board. Cover with a dry cloth; let stand 5 to 15 minutes.
Wash and grease bowl; set aside. Grease 2 large baking sheets; set aside.
Adding flour as necessary, knead dough until smooth, about 10 minutes.
Place in greased bowl, turning to grease all sides. Cover and let rise in a
warm place until doubled in bulk, about 2 hours. Punch down dough; divide
into 4 equal parts. Shape each into a round ball. Place 2 balls of dough on
each prepared baking sheet. Let rise in a warm place until doubled in bulk,
45 to 60 minutes. Preheat oven to 375°F (190°C). Bake 25 minutes or until
loaves sound hollow when tapped with your fingers. Cool on a rack. Makes
4 loaves.

Rye-Meal Bread

Ruisleipä—Finland

A sourdough version of this bread is popular in Finland and Sweden.

    1 envelope active dry yeast (¼ ounce)
    2 teaspoons sugar
    1¼ cups warm water (110°F, 45°C)
    1½ teaspoons salt
    2 teaspoons shortening, melted
    1½ cups rye meal or whole-wheat flour
    1¾ to 2 cups all-purpose or bread flour
    1 tablespoon butter, melted

In a large bowl, stir yeast and sugar into warm water; let stand 5 minutes to soften. Stir in salt and shortening. Add rye meal or whole-wheat flour; beat until smooth. Adding 1 cup at a time, beat in enough all-purpose or bread flour to make a stiff dough. Turn out onto a lightly floured board. Cover with a dry cloth; let stand 5 to 15 minutes. Wash and grease bowl; set aside. Grease a large baking sheet; set aside. Adding flour as necessary to prevent sticking, knead dough until smooth, about 10 minutes. Place in greased bowl, turning to grease all sides. Cover and let rise in a warm place until doubled in bulk, about 2 hours. Punch down dough; shape into a ball. Flatten to a round loaf, 10 inches in diameter. Pressing with your fingers and thumbs, make a hole in center. Stretch until hole is 2 inches in diameter. Place shaped loaf on prepared baking sheet. Cover and let dough rise until doubled in bulk, about 1 hour. Preheat oven to 375°F (190°C). Use tines of a fork to make punctures over top of loaf. Bake 30 to 35 minutes or until golden brown. Brush top of hot loaf with butter. Cool on a rack. To serve, cut loaf into wedges. Split wedges horizontally. Makes 1 large loaf.

Danish Pumpernickel

Rugbrød—Denmark

This bread is close-textured, grainy, and full of hearty flavor.

2 envelopes active dry yeast (¼ ounce each)
1½ cups warm water (110°F, 45°C)
½ cup dark molasses
3 tablespoons butter, melted
2 tablespoons caraway seeds
1 teaspoon salt
2 cups rye meal or cracked wheat
3 to 4 cups all-purpose or bread flour

In a large bowl, stir yeast into warm water; let stand 5 minutes to soften. Stir in molasses, butter, caraway seeds, and salt. Stir in rye meal or cracked wheat. Let stand 10 minutes. Adding 1 cup at a time, beat in enough flour to make a stiff dough. Turn out onto a lightly floured board. Cover with a dry cloth; let stand 5 to 15 minutes. Wash and grease bowl; set aside. Grease two 9 x 5-inch loaf pans; set aside. Adding flour as necessary, knead dough until smooth, about 10 minutes. Place in greased bowl, turning to grease all sides. Cover and let rise in a warm place until doubled in bulk, about 2 hours. Punch down dough; divide in half. Shape each half into a loaf. Place loaves, seam-side down, in prepared pans. Cover and let rise until doubled in bulk, about 1 hour. Preheat oven to 350°F (175°C). Brush tops of loaves with water, then bake 40 to 45 minutes or until loaves sound hollow when tapped with your fingers. Turn out of pans; cool on a rack. Makes 2 loaves.

Swedish Limpa
Limpa—Sweden

The blended flavors of orange and anise make this rye bread different and special.

1 envelope active dry yeast (¼ ounce)
¼ cup warm water (110°F, 45°C)
2 cups milk, scalded, cooled
½ cup dark molasses
½ cup vegetable oil
½ cup packed brown sugar
1½ teaspoons salt
1½ teaspoons caraway seeds
1½ teaspoons fennel seeds
1½ teaspoons anise seeds
Grated peel of 1 orange
1½ cups stirred rye flour
5 to 6 cups all-purpose or bread flour

In a large bowl, stir yeast into warm water; let stand 5 minutes to soften. Stir in milk, molasses, oil, brown sugar, and salt. Crush caraway seeds, fennel seeds, and anise seeds in a mortar and pestle, or pour into a plastic bag and pound with a hammer. Add crushed seeds, orange peel, and rye flour to yeast mixture. Beat until smooth. Adding 1 cup at a time, beat in enough all-purpose or bread flour to make a stiff dough. Turn out onto a lightly floured board. Cover with a dry cloth; let stand 5 to 15 minutes. Wash and grease bowl; set aside. Grease 2 round 8- or 9-inch cake pans; set aside. Adding flour as necessary, knead dough until smooth, about 10 minutes. Place in greased bowl, turning to grease all sides. Cover and let rise in a warm place until doubled in bulk, 1 to 1½ hours. Punch down dough; divide in half. Shape each half into a round loaf. Place loaves, seam-side down, in prepared pans. Cover and let rise until doubled in bulk, about 1 hour. Preheat oven to 375°F (190°C). Bake 35 minutes or until loaves sound hollow when tapped with your fingers. Turn out of pans; cool on a rack. Makes 2 loaves.

Whole-Wheat Bread

Hvetekake—Norway

Norwegians prefer whole-grain breads such as this for sandwiches.

> 1 envelope active dry yeast (¼ ounce)
> 2 cups warm water (110°F, 45°C)
> 2 tablespoons granulated sugar
> 3 cups all-purpose or bread flour
> ½ cup packed brown sugar
> ½ cup water
> 3 tablespoons butter, melted
> 2 teaspoons salt
> 3 to 3½ cups whole-wheat flour
> Water

In a large bowl, stir yeast into 2 cups warm water; let stand 5 minutes to soften. Stir in granulated sugar and all-purpose or bread flour. Beat until smooth. Cover and let rise in a warm place, 30 minutes or until bubbles begin to form. In a small bowl, stir brown sugar into ½ cup water until dissolved. Stir in butter and salt. Stir brown-sugar mixture into yeast mixture. Gradually stir in enough whole-wheat flour to make a stiff dough. Lightly sprinkle a board with whole-wheat flour. Turn dough out onto floured board. Cover with a dry cloth; let stand 5 to 15 minutes. Wash and grease bowl; set aside. Grease 2 round 8- or 9-inch cake pans, 9 x 5-inch loaf pans, or large baking sheets; set aside. Adding flour as necessary, knead dough until smooth, about 10 minutes. Place in greased bowl, turning to grease all sides. Cover and let rise in a warm place until doubled in bulk, 1½ to 2 hours. Punch down dough; divide in half. Shape each half into a round, oblong, or French-bread shape. Place shaped loaves in pans or on baking sheets. Cover and let rise until doubled in bulk, about 1 hour. Preheat oven to 350°F (175°C). Brush tops of raised loaves with water. Bake 40 to 45 minutes or until loaves sound hollow when tapped with your fingers. Turn out of pans; cool on racks. Makes 2 loaves.

Country Oat Loaf
Havremelsbrød—Denmark

Rolled-oats topping was a special touch from a Danish farmwoman.

2 cups milk, boiling
1 cup uncooked rolled oats
2 tablespoons butter
¼ cup dark molasses
1 teaspoon salt
1 envelope active dry yeast (¼ ounce)
¼ cup warm water (110°F, 45°C)
5 to 5½ cups all-purpose or bread flour
Egg Glaze (page 241)
Rolled oats

In a large bowl, pour boiling milk over 1 cup rolled oats. Stir in butter, molasses, and salt; let stand 30 minutes. In a small bowl, stir yeast into warm water; let soften 5 minutes. Stir into oats mixture. Adding 1 cup at a time, beat in enough flour to make a stiff dough. Turn out onto a lightly floured board. Cover with a dry cloth; let stand 5 to 15 minutes. Wash and grease bowl; set aside. Grease 2 round 9-inch cake pans; set aside. Adding flour as necessary, knead dough until smooth, about 10 minutes. Place in greased bowl, turning to grease all sides. Cover and let rise in a warm place until doubled in bulk, about 2 hours. Punch down dough; divide in half. Shape each half into a round loaf. Place loaves, seam-side down, in prepared pans. Cover and let rise until doubled in bulk, about 1 hour. Brush loaves with Egg Glaze, then sprinkle them heavily with uncooked rolled oats. Preheat oven to 375°F (190°C). Bake 35 to 45 minutes or until loaves sound hollow when tapped with your fingers. Turn out of pans; cool on a rack. Makes 2 loaves.

Danish Pastry

WINDOW SHOPPING IN DENMARK can send a pastry addict into euphoria! Shelves in the windows of every baker's shop are filled with variation upon variation of treats made with sweet, flaky, yeast-risen Danish Pastry Dough. Danes call it *Vienna Bread* or *Wienerbrød*. Germans and Austrians call it *Copenhagen Pastry*.

Danish pastry is made by repeatedly rolling and folding lightly sweetened, cardamom-flavored yeast dough and butter. This produces layer upon layer of thin, buttery, crisp pastry. As you prepare the pastry, keep the dough cold. Be sure to include the chilling steps between each rolling and folding step. Chilled dough is easier to handle, and during the chilling, you can relax. A marble rolling pin will hold the cold and because of its weight, make your job of rolling easier.

For perfect Danish pastry, use the best grade of butter you can purchase. Unsalted, Grade AA butter gives the finest results, but lightly salted butter can be used. Rolled butter, which comes in one-pound blocks and is wrapped in a single piece of paper, is a lower-grade butter. It has more liquid incorporated with the fat. It will not make good Danish pastry.

The recipe for Danish Pastry Dough is used in all but one of the following variations. When only half of the dough is used, wrap the remaining dough in plastic wrap and store it in the refrigerator. Use it within four or five days.

Bear Claws
Wienerbrøds Kamme—Denmark

The literal translation is "Danish pastry combs."

1 recipe Danish Pastry Dough (page 255)
1 recipe Vanilla Buttercream (page 254)
1 recipe Almond Buttercream (page 260)
Water
1 cup pearl sugar (page XVII) or coarsely crushed sugar cubes
1 cup sliced almonds
1 recipe Almond Icing (page 257) if desired

Divide pastry into 4 equal pieces. On a lightly floured board, roll 1 piece into a 12-inch square. Spread one-fourth of Vanilla Buttercream down center third of pastry; top with one-fourth of Almond Buttercream. Fold right and left thirds over center. Pinch edges of pastry to seal. Lightly roll crosswise with a rolling pin until pastry is 5 to 6 inches wide. Cut dough crosswise into 2-inch slices. On long side of each 2-inch slice, cut 4 parallel slashes, equal distance apart, to within ½ inch of other edge. Repeat with remaining dough. Pour water 2 inches deep into a medium bowl. Combine sugar and almonds in another medium bowl. Quickly dip top side of each Bear Claw in and out of water, then into sugar mixture. Arrange on an ungreased baking sheet, coated-side up, curving slightly to open claws. Cover with plastic wrap; let rise 45 minutes. Preheat oven to 400°F (205°C). Remove plastic wrap. Bake 13 to 15 minutes or until golden brown. Cool on a rack. Drizzle with Almond Icing, if desired. Makes 24 Bear Claws.

Pearl sugar is available in food shops that have Scandinavian ingredients and in some cake decorating stores. It is imported from Sweden and is usually sold in one-pound or smaller bags. If you cannot find pearl sugar, substitute crushed sugar cubes or loaf sugar.

Snails

Snegle—Denmark

These are similar to cinnamon rolls.

1 recipe Danish Pastry Dough (page 255)
½ recipe Vanilla Buttercream (page 254)
1 recipe Almond Buttercream (page 260)
1 egg, beaten
1 recipe Coffee Glaze (page 263)

Divide pastry in half; refrigerate 1 piece. On a lightly floured board, roll remaining half into a 16 x 8-inch rectangle. Spread with half of Vanilla Buttercream. Top with half of Almond Buttercream. Starting on a long side, roll up jelly-roll fashion. Cut roll crosswise into 16 slices. Place each slice in a paper muffin-cup liner. Arrange filled liners on an ungreased baking sheet. Repeat with remaining dough. Cover and let rise in a warm place, 45 minutes. Preheat oven to 400°F (205°C). Brush pastries with beaten egg. Bake 12 to 15 minutes or until lightly browned. Brush hot baked pastries with Coffee Glaze. Makes 32 Snails.

Vanilla Buttercream
Vanille Smørcreme—Denmark

Use this sweet mixture as a filling and an icing for Danish pastry.

    ½ cup butter, room temperature
    1 cup powdered sugar
    ½ teaspoon vanilla extract

Blend butter and powdered sugar. Blend in vanilla. Makes about 1 cup.

Danish Pastry Dough
Weinerbrød—Denmark

*This flaky yeast pastry is known as "Copenhagen dough" in Germany and
Austria.*

> 1¼ cups unsalted grade AA butter, chilled
> 2 envelopes active dry yeast (¼ ounce each)
> ¼ cup warm water (110°F, 45°C)
> ½ cup evaporated milk, room temperature
> 2 eggs, room temperature
> ½ teaspoon crushed cardamom seeds, if desired
> 1 teaspoon salt
> ¼ cup sugar
> 2½ to 3 cups all-purpose flour

Place butter between two 12-inch squares of plastic wrap. Pound with a rolling pin until butter can be shaped without breaking. Leaving butter between
pieces of plastic wrap, roll to a 10 x 8-inch rectangle; refrigerate. Place a
36 x 24-inch breadboard in refrigerator or freezer to chill, or place 2 large
baking sheets in freezer to chill. In a large bowl, stir yeast into warm water;
let stand 5 minutes to soften. Stir in milk, eggs, cardamom (if desired), salt,
and sugar until blended. Add 2½ cups flour all at once. Beat until dough
comes away from side of bowl. Add more flour as needed to make a stiff
dough. Or, pour yeast mixture into a food processor fitted with a metal
blade. Add milk, eggs, cardamom (if desired), salt, and sugar; process until
blended. Add 2½ cups flour; process until dough comes away from side of
bowl. Add more flour if needed. Dough will be soft, glossy, and smooth.
Grease a large bowl; place dough in bowl, turning to grease all sides. Cover
with plastic wrap; refrigerate 30 minutes to let dough relax. Dust chilled
breadboard with flour, or place chilled baking sheets on a board, 2 to 3
minutes, to chill board; dust chilled board with flour. *To roll dough:* Turn
dough out onto floured board. Dust ball of dough with flour, then roll into
an 18 x 12-inch rectangle. Remove plastic wrap from chilled butter. Place

chilled butter crosswise on 1 end of pastry, about 1 inch from all 3 edges. Fold other half of dough over butter. Press out any air bubbles; pinch edges to seal. Roll out dough to make as large a square as possible, but at least 20 inches square. Puncture bubbles as they form; pinch dough to seal any holes that form. Fold pastry square in thirds, folding right and left thirds over center. Seal layers together by pressing with side of your hands, or lightly roll with a rolling pin. If necessary, dust board and dough lightly with flour to prevent sticking. Again, fold dough in thirds; press layers together. Wrap folded dough in plastic wrap; refrigerate 15 to 30 minutes to let dough relax and chill. Roll chilled dough to make a 24-inch square. Fold into thirds; press or roll lightly to seal layers. Again fold in thirds. Wrap in plastic wrap and refrigerate 15 to 30 minutes. For a third time, repeat rolling, folding, and chilling. Wrapped dough may be stored in refrigerator 4 to 5 days. Makes about 1½ pounds dough.

Almond Icing

Mandelglasur—Denmark

Use this smooth icing on Danish pastry, cookies, and cupcakes.

1 cup powdered sugar
2 tablespoons water
1 teaspoon vegetable oil
½ teaspoon almond extract

In a small bowl, blend powdered sugar with water, oil, and almond extract until smooth. Add more water if necessary to make an icing thin enough to drizzle. Makes about ½ cup.

Marzipan Kringle
Kringle—Denmark

So crisp, light, and rich, you can serve this as a birthday cake for a Danish pastry addict!

> 1 envelope active dry yeast (¼ ounce)
> ½ cup warm milk (110°F, 45°C)
> 1 tablespoon sugar
> 3 egg yolks, slightly beaten
> 1 cup whipping cream
> 3½ cups all-purpose flour
> ¼ cup sugar
> 1 teaspoon salt
> ½ cup butter, chilled
> Marzipan Filling (see below)
> ¼ cup pearl sugar (page XVII), coarsely crushed sugar cubes, or
>   granulated sugar
> 1 egg white, slightly beaten
> ¼ cup sliced almonds

Marzipan Filling
> 1 package almond paste (8 ounces)
> ½ cup chopped almonds
> ½ cup sugar
> 1 egg white
> 1 teaspoon ground cinnamon
> 1 teaspoon almond extract

In a medium bowl, combine yeast, milk, 1 tablespoon sugar, egg yolks, and cream; let stand 10 minutes. In a large bowl, blend flour, ¼ cup sugar, and salt. Cut in butter until pieces are the size of kidney beans. Add yeast mixture; fold in only until dry ingredients are moistened. Cover with plastic wrap; refrigerate 12 to 24 hours. Prepare Marzipan Filling. Turn dough out onto a lightly floured board; dust dough with flour. Using a rolling pin, pound dough until smooth and ¾ inch thick. Roll dough to a 24-inch square. If necessary, fold in half, then knead 4 or 5 times to make dough easier to roll. Spread filling to within 1 inch of edges. Roll up tightly, jelly-roll fashion. Sprinkle work surface with pearl sugar, crushed sugar cubes, or granulated sugar. Roll dough in sugar. Brush surface of dough with egg white, then roll in sugar again. Generously grease a large baking sheet. Shape dough into a large pretzel by laying rolled dough on prepared baking sheet, curved like a *U,* with ends even. About 5 inches from ends, loop sides of *U* around each other. Tuck ends under closed part of *U.* Again brush with egg white; sprinkle with almonds. Cover and let rise in a warm place, 40 minutes. Kringle will not double in bulk. Preheat oven to 375°F (190°C). Bake 25 to 30 minutes or until golden brown. Makes 1 large kringle or 12 servings.

Marzipan Filling

Break almond paste into small pieces. In a medium bowl, combine almond-paste pieces and remaining ingredients. Press with the back of a wooden spoon until blended.

Almond Buttercream

Mandel Smørcreme—Denmark

Almond is a favorite filling flavor for Danish pastry.

¼ cup almond paste
¼ cup butter
½ cup powdered sugar

In a medium bowl or in a food processor fitted with a metal blade, blend almond paste, butter, and powdered sugar until smooth. Makes about ¾ cup.

Boston Cake

Smørkage—Denmark

In Finland and Sweden this is known as "Bostonkakku."

1 recipe Danish Pastry Dough (page 255)
⅓ cup sugar
2 tablespoons ground cinnamon
1 recipe Vanilla Buttercream (page 254)
1 recipe Coffee Glaze (page 263)

Roll out pastry to as large a rectangle as your work surface will allow, preferably 36 x 20 inches, but at least a 20-inch square. If pastry is hard to roll, let it rest 30 seconds, then continue rolling. In a small bowl, blend sugar and cinnamon. Spread dough with Vanilla Buttercream to within 1 inch of edges, then sprinkle with sugar-cinnamon mixture. Beginning on a long side, roll up jelly-roll fashion. Cut roll into 8 equal pieces. Generously butter a 2½- to 3-quart ring mold or tube pan. Place dough cut-side down in pan, spacing evenly to allow for rising. Cover and let rise 1½ to 2 hours or until pastry is light and puffy. Preheat oven to 350°F (175°C). Bake 45 to 55 minutes or until golden brown and a skewer inserted 2½ inches from center comes out clean. Cool on a rack 5 minutes, then turn out of pan. Drizzle with Coffee Glaze. Makes about 24 servings.

Danish Pastry Braid
Wienerfletning—Denmark

Folding the dough makes this look like a braid—although it isn't one.

½ recipe Danish Pastry Dough (page 255)
½ recipe Vanilla Buttercream (page 254)
½ recipe Almond Buttercream (page 260)
1 egg, slightly beaten
1 recipe Almond Icing (page 257)
Toasted sliced almonds

On a lightly floured surface, roll out pastry to a 24 x 8-inch rectangle. Cut in half, making two 12 x 8-inch pieces. Place each on a separate ungreased baking sheet. Spread half of Vanilla Buttercream lengthwise down the center third of each pastry; top with half of Almond Buttercream. With a sharp knife, make slashes at a 45-degree angle from buttercream mixture to outer edges of pastry, at 1-inch intervals. Alternately fold strips over filling in a criss-cross fashion, to give pastry a braided appearance. Cover and let rise 1 hour at room temperature. Preheat oven to 400°F (205°C). Brush with beaten egg. Bake 13 to 15 minutes or until golden brown and crisp. While still warm, decorate with Almond Icing and almonds. Makes 12 servings.

Coffee Glaze
Kaffeglasur—Denmark

Use this glaze on Danish pastry, cinnamon rolls, or Kaffekrans (Cinnamon Coffee Ring, page 237).

  1 cup powdered sugar
  2 tablespoons hot strong coffee or 1 teaspoon instant coffee dissolved
    in 2 tablespoons hot water
  2 tablespoons butter, room temperature

In a small bowl, blend powdered sugar, coffee, and butter until smooth. Makes about ½ cup.

Coffeetable Celebrations

MENU

FIRST COURSE:

Holiday Bread (page 240)

Cardamom Coffee Braid (page 242)

SECOND COURSE:

Lingonberry Spice Cake (page 222)

THIRD COURSE:

Strawberry Cream Cake (page 157)

Marzipan Kringle (page 258)

COOKIES:

Finnish Nut Logs (page 277)

Raspberry Ribbons (page 278)

Spritz (page 275)

Butter Cookie Shells (page 276)

Spicy Christmas Pigs (page 269)

Rosettes (page 281)

Krumbcakes (page 280)

Poor Men (page 273)

IN SCANDINAVIA, the term "coffeetable" refers to a three-course refreshment table. Coffeetables are appropriate for an open house, wedding, engagement, birthday, nameday, confirmation or baptism, anniversary, Christmas, St. Lucia Day, or in honor of a visiting dignitary. Coffeetables are offered in public places, too, such as at the opening of a new business, after a public meeting, or following the performance of an artist. Coffeetables are served at any time of day or night.

If you are served a coffeetable in Finland at Christmastime, you will have seven courses of baked goods and sip at least four cups of coffee.

The most formal coffeetable must include at least seven items. There are three courses: bread with cheese or open-face sandwiches; unfrosted cake such as pound cake; and a fruit- or cream-filled cake or torte. At least four varieties of cookies complete the menu. You are always served several cups of richly brewed coffee in cups slightly larger than demitasse cups. For large groups, coffeetables are reduced to a simpler menu—bread, cookies, and perhaps some small tarts.

The breads served will vary, depending on where you are in Scandinavia. Open-face sandwiches are common in Denmark. In Norway, *lefse,* a pliable, flat, potato bread, often appears on the coffeetable. In Finland, *pulla,* a cardamom-flavored braid, is always present.

When serving yourself, begin with the least sweet of the items offered. With the first cup of coffee, select a piece of bread with a thin slice of cheese or a sandwich. With the second cup of coffee, take the unfrosted cake. With the third cup of coffee, help yourself to the filled cake or torte.

During the holiday season, sweet breads, cakes, cookies, and pastries are served. For Christmas, *Glögg,* a hot, spiced-wine punch may be served as a substitute for coffee.

In this menu, prepare one item from each of the the first three courses and make four different cookies.

Scandinavian Cookies

COOKIES! COOKIES! COOKIES! Self-respecting Scandinavian bakers will not lay down their wooden spoons until they have baked at least a dozen varieties for Christmas! But that is not the only time they bake cookies. Scandinavians enjoy informal entertaining, and are always ready for the unexpected visitor.

Several years ago we visited a farm family who stored butter cookies in the cool depths of their well during the summertime. Today, most families keep a supply of cookies in the freezer. You can purchase a great variety of cookies and fancy little cakes at the confectioner's and in the market. They are expensive, however, so most homemakers prefer to make their own.

During the summer in Scandinavia, it is light day and night. Therefore, any time can be coffee time—the time for getting together. A guest will never protest more than twice if asked to remove an overcoat and come in. The encounter might be as follows: "Please come in and have a cup of coffee." "Honestly, I couldn't." "But really, you must try a little piece!" "Well, just a little. . . . "

Butter cookies are my favorite. With slight variations, they are common to all Scandinavian countries. In fact, it is difficult to distinguish between countries, because they cross borders. Because they are so similar, I've given you a basic dough and several variations.

By far the most popular cookie throughout the year is the ginger cookie or *pepperkaker*. There are various spellings of the same cookie throughout Scandinavia. Spicy Christmas Pigs are technically ginger cookies. These cookies appear in bakeries and food markets all over Finland beginning in Advent. When children see these decorated, pig-shaped cookies, they know the Christmas season has arrived. The symbolism of the pig probably dates back to when each family raised a pet pig for the holiday meals. The cookies are decorated with the word *Nissu* or *Nassu* in icing, or they can be decorated with a child's name.

The same dough can be cut into other shapes. The Dala horse, from Dalarna, Sweden, is a classic Christmas cookie shape. Or, a host may pipe the names of his or her dinner guests on heart-shaped ginger cookies and use them as place cards. Gingerbread men and ladies, Christmas trees, Santa Clauses, and roosters are other classic shapes for these cookies.

Spicy Christmas Pigs

Nissu Nassu—Finland

When children see these pig-shaped cookies in Finnish bakeries, they know Christmas is coming!

⅔ cup butter, room temperature
¾ cup packed brown sugar
1 tablespoon ground cinnamon
2 teaspoons ground ginger
1½ teaspoons ground cloves
1½ teaspoons baking soda
2½ cups all-purpose flour
¼ cup water

Royal Icing
1 egg white
3 to 4 cups unsifted powdered sugar
1 to 2 tablespoons water

In a medium bowl or food processor fitted with a metal blade, mix butter, brown sugar, cinnamon, ginger, cloves, baking soda, flour, and water until blended and dough forms a smooth ball. If dough is very soft, refrigerate 30 minutes. Preheat oven to 375°F (190°C). Lightly grease a large baking sheet; set aside. On a lightly floured surface, roll dough ⅛ inch thick. Cut with a pig or other animal-shaped cookie cutter. Place cut-out cookies on prepared baking sheet. Bake 7 to 10 minutes or until crisp and lightly browned. Cool on a rack. Prepare Royal Icing. To decorate cookies, pipe on features of animals or other decorative designs. With icing, write *Nissu* on half of pig-shaped cookies and *Nassu* on the other half. Or, write family names or names of guests and use as placecards, if desired. Makes 60 to 70 cookies.

Royal Icing

In a medium bowl, beat egg white until frothy; gradually beat in powdered sugar, making an icing thin enough to drizzle. Or spoon icing into a pastry bag fitted with a thin writing tip. Press icing out to write names.

Vanilla Wreaths

Vanillekranser—Denmark

These delicate, buttery cookie rings are traditionally served at Christmas.

2 cups all-purpose flour
1 cup sugar
⅛ teaspoon baking powder
Pinch salt
1 cup butter, room temperature
1 egg, slightly beaten
½ cup blanched almonds, ground
1 teaspoon vanilla extract

Lightly grease a large baking sheet or line a sheet with parchment paper; set aside. Preheat oven to 375°F (190°C). In a large bowl, combine flour, sugar, baking powder, and salt; blend. Stir in butter with a fork until mixture is crumbly. Add egg, almonds, and vanilla; blend until dough is smooth and pliable. Refrigerate 30 minutes. Spoon dough into a cookie press. Attach ¼-inch tube tip. Press dough through tube onto a lightly floured board, making long strips. Cut in 5-inch lengths. Working with 1 piece at a time, place on prepared baking sheet, overlapping ends to make small circles. Do not pinch ends together. Bake in preheated oven 8 minutes or until lightly browned. Cool on a rack. Makes about 96 cookies.

Gingerbread Cookies

Pepperkaker—Norway

These cookies are popular all year in Scandinavia, but are always present at Christmastime.

⅔ cup butter, room temperature
¾ cup packed light-brown sugar
3 to 4 tablespoons water
2 tablespoons dark molasses
2 cups all-purpose flour
1 tablespoon ground cinnamon
1½ teaspoons ground cloves
1 teaspoon ground ginger
1 teaspoon ground cardamom
1 teaspoon grated lemon peel
1 teaspoon baking soda

In large bowl of electric mixer, cream butter and brown sugar until blended. Beat in 3 tablespoons water and molasses until smooth. In a medium bowl, combine flour, cinnamon, cloves, ginger, cardamom, lemon peel, and baking soda. Gradually stir into molasses mixture to make a stiff dough. Add remaining 1 tablespoon of water, if necessary, to shape dough into a ball. Wrap ball of dough in plastic wrap. Refrigerate 30 minutes. Preheat oven to 350°F (175°C). Line baking sheets with parchment paper, or grease lightly. On a lightly floured surface, roll dough ⅛ to ¼ inch thick. Cut into hearts, gingerbread men and ladies, or other shapes. Arrange on prepared baking sheets. Bake 10 to 12 minutes or until firm, but not browned. Cool on a rack. Makes about 48 cookies.

Baked goods brown more evenly and cleanup is easier when you cover baking sheets with parchment paper rather than greasing them.

Poor Men

Fattigmandbakkelse—Norway

Delicate, crisp, diamond-shaped delicacies.

2 eggs
2 tablespoons whipping cream
1 teaspoon vanilla extract
3 tablespoons granulated sugar
1½ cups all-purpose flour
Fat for deep-frying
Powdered sugar

In a large bowl, beat eggs, cream, and vanilla until blended. Stir in granulated sugar and flour, making a stiff dough. On a lightly floured board, roll out half of dough, ⅛ inch thick. Cut dough in 1-inch strips; cut strips, diagonally, into 2½ inch pieces. Make a slit 1-inch long down center on the diagonal between 2 corners farthest apart. Pull 1 end through slit to make a twist out of the dough. Pour oil 2 inches deep into a medium saucepan. Place over medium heat. Heat to 375°F (190°C). Use a slotted spoon to lower twisted dough carefully into hot fat. Cook about 2 minutes or until golden brown on both sides. Drain on paper towels. When cool, dust with powdered sugar. Serve or freeze in a container with a tight-fitting lid. Makes 48 cookies.

Butter Cookie Dough

Pikkuleipienperustaikina—Finland

❊

This basic dough can be shaped in many ways to make Scandinavian holiday cookies.

    1 cup butter (2 sticks), room temperature
    ½ cup sugar
    1 egg, slightly beaten
    2½ cups all-purpose flour
    1 teaspoon vanilla extract
    ¼ teaspoon salt
    1 to 2 teaspoons water, if needed

In a medium bowl or in a food processor fitted with a metal blade, mix butter, sugar, egg, flour, vanilla, and salt until a smooth, pliable cookie dough forms. If mixture seems dry, work in 1 to 2 teaspoons water. Gather dough into a ball; knead slightly. Wrap in plastic wrap and refrigerate 30 minutes or until ready to use. Dough can be stored in refrigerator up to 1 week. Use the dough in the following recipes. Makes about 2 cups dough.

Spritz

Sprits—Sweden

Popular all year, but especially during the holidays.

Butter Cookie Dough (page 274)
Colored sugar

Preheat oven to 350°F (175°C). Do not refrigerate cookie dough. Fill a cookie press with dough as manufacturer directs. Select plate and fit onto press. Press dough onto an ungreased baking sheet. Sprinkle with colored sugar. Bake 10 to 12 minutes or just until cookies are firm and lightly browned around edges. Do not overbake. Cool on a rack. Makes about 100 cookies.

Butter Cookie Shells

Sandbakelser—Sweden

These look like they ought to have a filling, but they don't.

Butter Cookie Dough (page 274)
½ teaspoon almond extract

Preheat oven to 375°F (190°C). When preparing Butter Cookie Dough, add ½ teaspoon almond extract with vanilla. Refrigerate dough 30 minutes. Divide into fourths. On a lightly floured surface, roll 1 piece of dough into a rectangle, ⅛ inch thick. Arrange 12 *sandbakelser tins* (page XVII) close together. Carefully lift dough and place over tins, letting dough drape into tins. Roll a rolling pin across tops of tins to cut dough. Dip your fingers in flour, then press dough evenly into tins. Bake 12 to 15 minutes or until cookie shells are lightly browned. Cool on a rack. Serve open-side down. Makes 48 (2-inch) shells or 60 to 72 (1½-inch) shells.

Variation
Spicy Sandbakelser: Add ¼ teaspoon ground cardamom to Butter Cookie Dough.

Finnish Nut Logs

Pähkinäleivät—Finland

These nut-crusted, golden cookies are a year-round favorite in Finland.

Butter Cookie Dough (page 274)
1 egg
¼ cup finely chopped almonds
2 tablespoons sugar

Preheat oven to 350°F (175°C). Lightly grease a large baking sheet; set
aside. Divide cookie dough into fourths. Rolling each between your hands
and a lightly floured surface, shape into ropes, ½ inch thick. Cut crosswise
into 2-inch slices. In a small shallow dish, beat egg until well blended and
smooth. In another small bowl, combine almonds and sugar. Roll cookie
slices or logs first in beaten egg, then in sugar mixture. Place 2 inches apart
on prepared baking sheet. Bake 12 to 15 minutes or until lightly browned.
Cool on a rack. Makes about 48 cookies.

Raspberry Ribbons

Hindbærkager—Denmark

These jam-filled cookie ribbons are a quick way to add color to the cookie tray.

> Butter Cookie Dough (page 274)
> ½ cup raspberry jam or jelly
> ½ cup powdered sugar
> 2 tablespoons milk

Preheat oven to 375°F (190°C). Divide cookie dough into fourths. Rolling each between your hands and a lightly floured surface, shape into ropes, about ½ inch thick. Place ropes on an ungreased baking sheet about 2 inches apart. With side of your little finger, press a long groove down length of each strand. Bake 10 minutes. Spoon jam or jelly into groove. Bake 5 to 10 minutes longer or until edges are lightly browned. In a small bowl, beat powdered sugar and milk to make a glaze. Brush or drizzle glaze over hot cookies. Cut logs diagonally into 1-inch slices. Makes about 96 cookies.

Almond Cookies

Mandelkaker—Norway

These nut-topped cookies are used on coffeetables all year long.

Butter Cookie Dough (page 274)
1 teaspoon almond extract
36 pieces slivered almonds or 18 candied cherries, halved
½ cup powdered sugar
2 tablespoons whipping cream or evaporated milk

Preheat oven to 350°F (175°C). When preparing Butter Cookie Dough, add 1 teaspoon almond extract with vanilla. Shape dough into 1-inch balls. Arrange on an ungreased baking sheet, 1 inch apart. Press a piece of almond or a halved cherry into center of each cookie. Bake 12 to 15 minutes, just until cookies are firm and beginning to brown around edges. Cool on a rack. In a small bowl, blend powdered sugar and cream or evaporated milk to make a thin icing. Drizzle icing over nut or fruit on each cookie. Makes about 36 cookies.

Krumbcakes

Krumkaker—Norway

These delicate, crisp cookies are a traditional Norwegian holiday treat.

> 1 cup sugar
> 2 eggs
> ½ cup butter, melted
> ⅔ cup milk
> 1⅓ cups all-purpose flour
> 1 teaspoon crushed cardamom seeds
> Water, if necessary

In a medium bowl, combine sugar, eggs, and butter. Use a whisk to beat in milk until mixture is blended and smooth. Stir in flour until blended. Stir in cardamom. Preheat *krumkaker iron* (page XVI) over medium heat until a drop of water sizzles when dropped on top. Open iron; lightly brush inside top and bottom with shortening, oil, or melted butter. Spoon 1 tablespoon batter onto center of hot iron. Close iron. Bake about 1 minute on each side or until cookie is lightly browned. Insert tip of a knife under cookie to remove from iron; roll hot cookie into a cigar or cone shape. Cool on a rack. Cookies become crisp as they cool. Repeat with remaining batter. If batter becomes thick, stir in water, 1 tablespoon at a time. Store in an airtight container. These freeze well. Makes 25 to 30 krumbcakes.

Rosettes

Rosettes—Sweden

Rosette irons come with interchangeable shapes.

2 eggs
2 teaspoons granulated sugar
¼ teaspoon salt
1 cup milk
1 cup all-purpose flour
Oil for deep-frying
Powdered sugar

In a small bowl, beat eggs, granulated sugar, salt, and milk with a whisk until blended. Beat in flour to make a smooth batter. Let stand 30 minutes. Pour oil 2 inches deep into a medium saucepan. Over medium heat, heat to 375°F (190°C). Place rosette iron into hot oil for 1 minute; shake off excess oil. Immediately dip into batter, being careful not to let batter come over top edge of iron. Immerse batter-covered iron into hot fat. Shake iron to loosen the rosette while immersed in hot oil. Fry about 1 minute or until golden brown. Use a slotted spoon to lift cooked rosette from hot oil. Drain on paper towels. To serve, dust with powdered sugar. Makes about 36 rosettes.

Blueberry Bars

Mustikkapiirakka—Finland

Delightful combination—lemon-accented blueberry filling and butter crust.

Butter Crust (see below)
2 cups fresh or frozen unsweetened blueberries
¼ cup sugar
1 tablespoon lemon juice
1 tablespoon grated lemon peel
2 tablespoons cornstarch
¼ teaspoon salt
1 tablespoon sugar

Butter Crust

2½ cups all-purpose flour
½ teaspoon baking powder
½ cup sugar
1 cup butter, room temperature
1 egg, slightly beaten

Prepare Butter Crust; refrigerate 30 minutes. In a medium saucepan, combine blueberries, ¼ cup sugar, lemon juice, lemon peel, cornstarch, and salt. Over low heat, stir until mixture is blended. Increase heat to medium. Stirring constantly, cook until thickened. Cool to room temperature. Preheat oven to 375°F (190°C). Butter a 13 x 9-inch baking pan; set aside. Divide chilled dough into three-fourths and one-fourth portions. On a lightly floured surface, roll out large portion to a 15 x 11-inch rectangle for bottom crust. Roll around rolling pin; unroll into prepared baking pan. Dough will cover bottom of pan and extend 1 inch up each side. Spoon cooled filling into pastry. Roll out reserved dough, ⅛-inch thick; cut into ½-inch strips. Criss-cross strips over blueberry filling to make a lattice top. Sprinkle with 1 tablespoon sugar. Bake 25 to 30 minutes or until lattice is golden brown. Cool to room temperature. To serve, cut into 3-inch squares. Makes 12 servings.

Butter Crust

In a large bowl, combine flour, baking powder, and sugar. Using an electric mixer or wooden spoon, blend in butter. Add egg and continue mixing until a pliable dough forms.

Chocolate-Dipped Orange Sticks

Orangesmåkager—Denmark

Delicately flavored with orange, these bar cookies are a holiday favorite in Denmark.

½ cup butter, softened
1½ cups all-purpose flour
¼ cup sugar
3 tablespoons grated orange peel
1 egg
4 ounces semisweet chocolate, melted

Lightly grease a large baking sheet; set aside. Preheat oven to 400°F (205°C). In a large bowl, blend butter into flour by pressing with the back of a spoon. Add sugar, orange peel, and egg; stir until a stiff dough forms. Refrigerate 20 minutes if dough is soft. On a lightly floured surface, roll dough out until it is ¼ inch thick. Cut into 2 x 1-inch bars. Place on prepared baking sheet, 1 inch apart. Bake 10 minutes or until lightly browned. Dip 1 end of each baked bar in melted chocolate. Place on waxed paper until chocolate has set. Makes about 40 cookies.

Index

Scandinavian Recipe Titles

Denmark

Finland

Beatrice Ojakangas is the author of more than twenty cookbooks, including *The Great Scandinavian Baking Book, Scandinavian Feasts, The Great Holiday Baking Book, Great Whole Grain Breads, Quick Breads,* and *Pot Pies* (all published by the University of Minnesota Press). Her articles have appeared in *Bon Appétit, Gourmet, Cooking Light, Cuisine,* and *Redbook,* and she has been a guest on television's *Baking with Julia Child* and *Martha Stewart's Living.* She lives in Duluth, Minnesota.